Prophetic Eyes

Kofi's View

By
Lester Wingate
Kofi
The Silent Preacher

Email: clariongate@msn.com
www.sankofastar.com

Acknowledgement

"flow with me"

The name "Kofi" bears the author's identity. Kofi simply means "Friday Born". It is the name I acquired in Ghana, West Africa. The revelation speaks that I was born on a Friday, a day of the Lord's crucifixion. It was a day that I will always remember. My beginning was the first day of my ending trapped in the womb of time waiting for redemption. In His death, I was the thief stripped, persecuted, dangling from my own cross on the right side of Him. It was the day I cried out, *"Lord have mercy on me"*. I died with Him; went to paradise with Him and experienced the power of His redemptive love. Then after three days of fellowship in His presence, I arose in the same resurrection power that raised Him from the dead. The graves were opened and the Saints arose. The curtain was rent in two, from heaven to earth. With the release of His Spirit descending upon me, He gave me the *"eyes of fire"*. It will always be a reminder of the day that I laid down my life for the sake of the calling.

In writing this book, it is important to discover the motivation behind the name. Simply, I was instructed! In a vision in the night, I heard the words spoken into my spirit, *"finish the book"*! It left me with no options; a summons served; my obedience was required. After years of feasting the finest of wheat, it is now time to stir up the gift for you who are waiting at the table. My waiting has been a journey; a journey into a deeper dimension of faith.

My accomplishments in life lie in the shadows of the pursuit of the Excellency of Christ in whom all things I consider lost for the sake of His righteousness. The Prophetic Word for *"this spiritual season"* required an urgency for this writing. The adversary has battled me to keep this book from reaching you. There is a voice speaking that can't be silenced or hindered beyond the time of delivery. I pray that the words captured between these pages will fall upon the fertility of your hearing.

A Time to Hear

America, we are in the midst of a spiritual crisis! What you see happening in the natural is a product of our spiritual decline. Our times are filled with turmoil and uncertainty; violence, anger, murder, hatred and decline in a changing social paradigm. In defense of our prosperity, we have neglected the compassion of love as the center of peace for our humanity. Wars, riots and spiritual unrest are indications of a seasonal change that is happening in our atmosphere. From the shores of America to the deserts of Egypt, the evolution of change is adding so much perplexity for our generations that are waiting for the manifestation of the *"true sons of God"*.

We have entered into a revolution that is changing our spiritual and social landscape and will realign our political alliances. What we are witnessing in our times is a fulfillment of prophecy accelerating to a conclusion of chaotic proportions. The Spirit of God is brooding upon the waters of our destiny to bring revelation of a future that is being weighed in the balance of God's prophetic intentions.

Authors Note

When I was a child, my Mother took me to a camp meeting in Norfolk, Virginia to see Oral Roberts. My sentiment at the time was Oral who? When we arrived, I was excited to see a tent, not knowing what was on the inside. I made the assumption I was attending a circus. It was a big tent; people were standing in line waiting to get in with a sense of excitement brewing in the atmosphere. I heard from a distance, music, the clapping of hands and an exuberance that was pulsating through the canvas. Like any kid, I could not wait to get inside. I expected to see lions, tigers, zebras, elephants and all kinds of exotic animals that I had read about in books and watched on the "Wild Kingdom". After waiting which seemed like an eternity, a gentleman came out and redirected the line to the side of the tent to expedite seating. He seated us near the front. How awesome! It was close enough for a bird's eye view of all the activity. I waited and waited before perplexity began to settle in. Where are the animals? I could smell the scent of sawdust on the ground and an aroma that was very vague to my senses. Not very long after we took our seats, the gentleman returned and escorted us to the rear of the tent, where there were no seats. I guess you can say we were seated standing.

After standing for nearly an hour, Oral Roberts was finally introduced and he began to sing a song that still resonates in my spirit:

> *The chimes of time ring out the news, another day is through. Someone slipped and fell, was that someone you? You may have longed for added strength your courage to renew. Do not be disheartened, I have news for you. It is no secret what God can do, what he's done for others he'll do for you. With arms wide open, he'll pardon you, it is no secret what God can do.*

> *There is no night for in his light you'll never walk alone. Always feel at home, wherever you may roam. There is no power can conquer you while God is on your side. Just take him at his promise, don't run away and hide. It is no secret what God can do, what he's done for others he'll do for you. With arms wide open he'll pardon you, it is no secret what God can do.*

His word in song came to me as a prelude into the times of a future destiny. It was a prophecy into my life; a destiny of a miraculous life in the Spirit. Just as Elijah, the time and season is for an appointed time. For what has been veiled in secrecy, God has ordained the *"set time"* for the manifestation of the fullness of His expectancy.

When Oral Roberts began to minister, he fascinated my imagination. What I did not realize then, I was witnessing someone who had a hidden life in the presence of God that produced grace for a public display of His glory. I witnessed the supernatural performance of healing, deliverance by the word of knowledge and the power of revelation that was beyond my capacity to comprehend. It was so powerful, it left an indelible impression upon my spirit and a thirst for something greater than I had ever experienced. I immediately became attracted to the supernatural possibilities that could transform weakness into strength, failure to hope, deaf to hearing, sight to the blind and death to resurrection. His testimony was a demonstration of ministry that went beyond just the preaching of words but penetrated deeper delivering an unequivocal performance of power by the Holy Spirit.

At the end of the service, there was an alter call. I stepped forward and came down with my Mother by my side. I remember to this day, he laid hands on me and prayed. He spoke a language I did not understand, but I do remember He asked me did I want to serve the Lord. I answered to the call; "yes".

Looking back, I can understand the motivation and vision that was in Mother's heart. She was looking for an answer that could only come through the power of God. She believed that He was no respecter of person neither was He a respecter of youth. She had come with a hope and offered me as a sacrifice for her generation. It was a hope beyond the limitations that had kept much of the Body of Christ in division, segregated with her generation being held hostage to the decisions and politics of man. It was a hope elevated above prejudice and the failing ethics of past generations that created an inequality even in the Kingdom of God.

At the beginning of every summer, my Mother would always send me to my grandfather's farm in South Carolina. It was a place secluded from my peers and surroundings of familiarity. I do not know whether the seclusion was to protect me from people or to protect people from me. This particular summer as I made the journey to the farm, the words of Oral Roberts were still echoing in my spirit. I distinctly remember, on a hot summer morning, I hid myself in a closet. I had hoped that God would do for me as a child what He did for Oral Roberts. I told God that I was not coming out until He blessed me! I had heard those words spoken from the testimony Oral had given under the tent. As a child, he went into the closet and had a spiritual encounter. He experienced the power of God touching him and caused a revolution in his life. I was not to be denied! I believed what He had done for

Oral Roberts, He would do the same for me. I cried out *"Lord I am not coming out of this closet until you bless me"*. Then I heard the voice of thunder! It was my Grandfather; *"get the mule and the plow"*. His name was Willie, Deacon Willie E. Ham. He was a farmer, businessman, community leader and a well respected citizen of faith. He taught me the ethics of work and the disciplines of belief required to reap the fruit of the mustard seed.

It has been only until recent years I rediscovered the testimony of my youth. What I asked for as a child, the season of it is now coming to pass. It has taken years of preparation and trials for the birthing of truth that speaks: *"there is no secret what God can do, what He has done for others, he will do for you"*. God is truly not a respecter of persons but only judges the conditions of the heart of man. I have faith in the prayers of Oral Roberts and the prayers of my parents that a hope would be realized.

I discovered that Oral Roberts was operating in a realm where religion can't take you. The performance of faith demonstrated in his life by the gifting of the Holy Spirit distinguished itself from the limited power of man's wisdom and talents. Despite our aspirations in life, we must become a servant to the passion at the core of our existence. God has appropriated vision in the heart of every man and will perform the works of His destiny. It is my prayer that in this hour, we are able to apprehend the revelations of our time and can apply our obedience and faith worthy of His gifts.

Sankofa

"Sankofa" symbolizes a mythic bird that flies forward while looking backward with an egg symbolic of the future in its mouth. Our future is embodied in our past laden with the sufferings of hope from generations that sacrificed in faith.

"Sankofa" teaches that we must go back to our roots, the place of our beginnings, reaching back to discover the best of what our past has to teach us. In order to achieve our full potential as we move forward, we must never forget the sacrifices of our Elders. The pathway of our destiny to recover whatever we have lost, forgotten, forgone or been stripped of can be reclaimed, revived, preserved and perpetuated for our future.

Publishers Note

MasterWorks BookMakers Publishing Company is a subsidiary of Shadow Ministries Inc. We are proud to publish spiritual writings that are relevant for our times. By divine enlightenment of the Holy Spirit through visions, dreams and revelation knowledge, the discovery of truth offers us insight into the spiritual dimension that has never before been revealed. It is the prevailing theme of MasterWorks to represent scripture accurately within the full context that it is written.

> *And we have the prophetic word confirmed, which you do well to heed as a light that shines in a dark place, until the day dawns and the morning star rises in your hearts; knowing this first, that no prophecy of Scripture is of any private interpretation, for prophecy never came by the will of man, but holy men of God spoke as they were moved by the Holy Spirit.*

2 Peter 1:19-21

The light that shines in darkness is the prophetic voice of the Spirit of Christ that speaks into our time and seasons to deliver prophetic instructions for God's intended purpose. *"Prophetic Eyes"* is a classic that satisfies the threshold to be a spark that ignites the flame of fire to bring spiritual revelation to the Body of Christ. As we discover truth, let the Spirit of God bring into obedience the actions of our faith to perform the works of His destiny.

Kofi

DEDICATION

To Cousin Doris
"A Message From Sam"

No More Power To Weep

Then David and the people who were with him lifted up their voices and wept until they had no more power to weep.

1 Samuel 30:4

You are never alone when night suddenly appears. Scripture says David and the people, "together", lifted up their voices and wept. The tears of the Saints are precious in the sight of God. He bottles them up and remembers the invisible wind that is drawn from our emotions. The wind has weeping power that blows from the depths of despair. It is a prelude into a deeper dimension of God's love for us as He ushers in a new day of revelation into our lives. From the tranquil winds of the morning breeze to the turbulence of angry seas, the newness of dew moistened with hope removes the liability of our defeats, sufferings, trials and our tears. In our seeking as we pursued the will of God in anguish of an unsettled heart, we often cried out *"how long, Lord how long"* only to be reminded that the season end of His word must come to pass. Remember, there is no more power in our tears! The wind has spoken beyond our despair words of hope refreshing to our dreams:

Remember not the former things neither consider the things of old. I will do a new thing. Shall you not know it? **Isaiah 43:18**

The wind is sent as an Angel of God always present and ready at the summons of His power. You see, it is God who controls the wind in our lives. He regulates the changing of our times from the blossoms of new beginnings to season's end of our faith. As the whitecaps of the waves of winter were beating upon the shores of our lives, I pondered the beginning of turmoil that had ushered in so much despair. In the silence of meditation, I considered its path from beginning until now.

The wind is a power that has no beginning and it has no end. From whence it cometh, I do not know. It travels from afar with the swiftness of an angel quietly waiting in the morning glow of day. At season's end when sunset appears, it returns laden with passengers traveling in the night. This I have discovered, God created the wind sent to divide the waters of our lives. From the beginning, He breathed into my hollow chambers the very essence of His life and I became a living soul. I inhaled this new given life with a cry; it was a shout of praise. The life I breathed in expired at the fulfillment of its purpose. At some point, in all our crossings we must exhale and yield to the power that controls the destiny of life. The measurement of time is judged and the curtain is drawn to an end. The end must always take the path back to its beginnings. No more choices to consider; just an undivided life of spirit sifted from the sands of time.

The wind that produced the God life in me is now silenced for a greater voice. The seeds of righteousness have been planted, nourished and now bears fruit of its kind. A new generation emerges as the old passes away. It is the fulfillment of the first command of God *"be fruitful and multiply; fill the earth and subdue it"*. God gave us His Spirit with power and authority of immeasurable dimensions to reproduce the essence of His image. It was the gift of His love burning as a flame of fire, waiting to rendezvous the fragrance of two seeking souls with flaming hearts. As doves secluded singing in the passion of night, we embraced in love, forever cherished until the dawning of light.

I discovered that the wind of life's creativity can only be controlled from within the power of our dreams and activated only by the power of our choices. Our choices have power that measure the days of our eternity. Choose life to live in the never ending days of His presence. From the sanctuary of His habitation kindled with the fire of His eternal love, His hidden chamber of refuge has become my dwelling place. In surrender, I bowed in benevolence descending from a shout of pure joy to a waning whisper of a still quiet voice. While weeping in humility with my heart panting in hope, I surrendered to embrace His waiting arms, disappeared into His bosom, raptured in His love.

Have you seen the dancing of the wind? Look at the leaves on the tree dancing in a collective celebration. It is a sign of change with a freedom that can't be ordered. The dancing of the wind reveals the wings of God. It is a time of rejoicing, a celebration of life. The transcended joy takes the form of angels wearing the garments of praise portraying His glory and rejoicing in an eternal celebration. Rejoice and again I say rejoice until the clouds of glory are lifted and together, we will bow in worship to the revelation of the King. With Angels bowing down before Him shouting Hosanna to the King of Kings, I released my tears as His joy filled my heart. From the altar of sacrifice to the pedestal before His throne, I entered into that place of ultimate surrender receiving my garment of humility and experienced the power of His love. If you only knew where I was, you would not shed another tear. No more weariness; no more sleepless nights, the sting of death has been removed.

It was then I discovered the sanctuary of God's *"amazing grace"* that perfected us in the penetrating life of faith. I encountered a power that spoke solace to my spirit. The wind of heaviness has now been replaced with the wind of joy. *No more power to weep!* At the rising of the sun, the clouds of joy clap their hands in ecstasy with resounding thunder trembling hearts from head to feet, awakening to the voice that says; *"Joy does come in the morning"*.

The eyes of night have given birth to the morning light. It is morning time; the winds have silenced and ushered in a new day. The rains of spring has arrived, flowers are blooming with trees swaying in the morning breeze. The birds are nesting repeating the cycle of life. The *"Bright and Morning Star"* has appeared reawakening the newness of faith. Take a deep breath; breathe in the silence of the wind. I have been ushered into that place called peace.

> *And nothing of theirs was lacking, either small or great, sons or daughters, spoil or anything which they had taken from them; David recovered all.* **1 Samuel 30:19**

Table of Contents

FORWARD

By Inez Ham Wingate

1 Corinthians 13

I dedicate this book to my dear late mother, the steward of my faith, Inez Ham Wingate. This article that she wrote was published June 1, 1996. She lived a life in the shadows of the cross humbled and submitted to the power of God's love. She preached love; she gave love; she loved love. She poured into my life the wisdom of ages and appropriated the gifting of discernment. She taught me humility and the ability to recognize the difference between natural things and the principles of God's spiritual Kingdom.

"The Greatest of These is Love"

¹If I speak in the tongues of men and of angels, but have not love, I am only a resounding gong or a clanging cymbal. ²If I have the gift of prophecy and can fathom all mysteries and all knowledge, and if I have a faith that can move mountains, but have not love, I am nothing. ³If I give all I possess to the poor and surrender my body to the flames, but have not love, I gain nothing.

⁴Love is patient, love is kind. It does not envy, it does not boast, it is not proud. ⁵It is not rude, it is not self-seeking, it is not easily angered, it keeps no record of wrongs. ⁶Love does not delight in evil but rejoices with the truth. ⁷It always protects, always trusts, always hopes, always perseveres.

⁸Love never fails. But where there are prophecies, they will cease; where there are tongues, they will be stilled; where there is knowledge, it will pass away. ⁹For we know in part and we prophesy in part, ¹⁰but when perfection comes, the imperfect disappears. ¹¹When I was a child, I talked like a child, I thought like a child, I reasoned like a child. When I became a man, I put childish ways behind me. ¹²Now we see but a poor reflection as in a mirror; then we shall see face to face. Now I know in part; then I shall know fully, even as I am fully known. ¹³And now these three remain: faith, hope and love. But the greatest of these is love.

1 Corinthians 13

The Supreme Good

Everyone has asked themselves the great question of old as well as modern day; *what is the supreme good?* You have life before you; only once can you live it. So what is the noblest object of desire or the *supreme gift to covet?*

Some of the popular religious groups have looked upon faith as the greatest, but we have just read that love is the greatest. It is not an oversight; Paul says "If I have all faith so that I could remove mountains and have not love I am nothing".

In the 13th verse Paul says "Now abideth faith, hope, and charity but the greatest of these is charity". Peter added to this by saying "above all things have fervent love among yourselves". John goes further saying, *"God is Love"*.

Then Paul adds again *"Love is the fulfilling of the law"*. Did you ever think what Paul meant by that? In those days men and women were trying to work their way to heaven by keeping the ten commandments and manufactured their own self-righteousness.

Christ said, *"I will show you a more simpler way; if you love, you will automatically fulfill the whole law"*. Take any of the commandments:

"Thou shall have no other God before me." If a man loves God you are not required to tell him that love is the fulfilling of that law.

"Take not His name in vain." Would you ever think of taking His name in vain if you really loved him?

"Remember the Sabbath day to keep it holy." Would you be glad to have one day of seven to dedicate exclusively to the object of your affection. Love would fulfill all of these laws regarding God's commandments.

And if he loved man you would not think of telling him *to* *"honor his father and mother"* because he would do nothing else. You would have to tell him *"not to kill"* and you could insult him if you tell him *"not to steal"* from one he loves. It also would be strange to tell him *"not to steal from his neighbor"* because if he loved him that would be the last thing that he would do.

You would never dream of urging him *"not to bear false witness against his neighbor"* because this too is the last thing that he would do.

Love is the fulfilling of the law. It is the rule for fulfilling all rules. It is the New Commandment for keeping all the Old Commandments. This is Christ's secret of a Christian life: *"by this shall all men know that ye are my disciples if ye have love one for the other"*.

Parting Words

Life's breath is only a moment in time. What we breathe in at some point in our lives will be reclaimed, refreshing the eternal winds of time. At the moment of life's expiration, there is a breath with a lasting voice that will forever be remembered in the archives of eternity. I heard that voice at my Mother's bedside when the trumpets were blowing in a serenade of despair as a prelude of a lasting joy waiting for the chariots to arrive. Mother echoed her parting words to me which I will share with you and will forever cherish:

BE CAREFUL!

Prophets Wisdom

We, as believers of the Body of Christ, have the awesome privilege of joining ranks in this hour to participate in the great events which are even now being birthed in the earth. The price is high yet the reward is of greater value than the human mind can calculate. If we are to move in these realms of power and authority, we must understand the order of "the House, the House of God, the House of Prayer" where heaven bows to the attraction of our prayers. The Church has been growing in stature, moving and reclaiming the teaching, pastoral, evangelistic, prophetic and apostolic ministries. We have seen this in part but the full complement is yet to be realized. We now stand at the brink of the true apostolic and prophetic ministries being unveiled and set in order as the foundation for all of the ministries to take their rightful place. The revelation of Jesus will manifest with power and authority fitly joining the body to flow in harmony under the authority of Christ.

Prophet Susan Chapman

Preface

 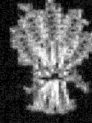

Looking Back

Blessed be the name of God forever and ever, For wisdom and might are His. 21 And He changes the times and the seasons; He removes kings and raises up kings; He gives wisdom to the wise And knowledge to those who have understanding. 22 He reveals deep and secret things; He knows what is in the darkness, And light dwells with Him. 23 " I thank You and praise You, O God of my fathers; You have given me wisdom and might, And have now made known to me what we asked of You, For You have made known to us the king's demand. **Daniel 2:20-23**

God is the giver of all gifts and talents that man possesses. Our gifting must possess power to bring life to our words. I have been told I have perfected the art of riddles. Is it a gift, talent or does it still remain a mystery? Hopefully by the end of this reading, you will decide. My style of writing is spontaneous at times; not able to contain the burst within me. It comes forth with its own uniqueness, struggling to conform to a set discipline of bringing shape and form to the image of my mind. All power comes from above from the Father of Lights who reveals all mysteries made known to man.

I discovered this truth early on in my walk of faith. As a Prophet, my life is a life of silence, the silence of words, always waiting for the revelation that speaks beyond any prior revelations and encounters. By the Word of God, I was commanded to leave my kindred to discover new territories off the beaten path. My journey took me to Ghana, West Africa, the gateway of my destiny. Under the authority of the Spirit, the reins that control our destiny will always lead us beyond our comfort level into new discoveries. Like John the Baptist, I was sent as a voice of one crying in the wilderness to usher in a new season of restoration.

This is the third book by Masterworks BookMakers Publishing Company, a proprietary owned exclusively by Shadow Ministries Inc. The previous two publications were targeted for the African Nations. The ministries of Emerging Destiny Intl., headquartered in Accra, Ghana West Africa, were established under the authority and guidance of the Holy Spirit working through Shadow Ministries. Shadow was established as a spiritual organism reclaiming the rights of the Believer. Churches were united with the common cause of bringing reclamation to the true apostolic order of God. By His grace, the ministry remains vibrate and growing by the guidance of the Holy Spirit.

As a veteran of war, I have a special interest in defending the honor and dignity of this nation through prayer and lifting up the banner of righteousness of Jesus Christ, who is the author of my existence. Scripture says we are to pray for our leaders and respect the powers that have rule over us. This is a truth. God's divine order is required at every level of authority; secular and spiritual.

> *Therefore I exhort first of all that supplications, prayers, intercessions, and giving of thanks be made for all men, ²for kings and all who are in authority, that we may lead a quiet and peaceable life in all godliness and reverence.*
> **1 Timothy 2:1-2**

A special thanks to Bishop Veronica Watson, the Prophet of God who poured an immeasurable flow of the anointing into my life that still sustains me. She is an anointed teacher of scripture and a powerful preacher that flows in revelation knowledge. The words she spoke to me in the midst of one of my greatest battles are still alive: *"You have more in your reserve than most people have in their tank."* It was through the mouth of this Prophet, I learned the revelation of the spiritual organism the Body of Christ is intended to be. I am honored to have feasted at the table with the Saints who brought acceptance of my gifts. I will be forever indebted to the trust of your stewardship.

I am very grateful for the foundational principles that were woven into my fabric at Jericho Ministries located in Landover, Maryland under the auspices of the late Bishop James Peeples Sr. and Apostle Betty Peeples. It was there I had my beginnings in ministry. Thank you for the seeds of righteousness deposited into my life. I will never forget.

To the Overcomer Ministries, I am very grateful for the lessons learned during my tenure as a servant to you. I will always remember the sacrifice of your labor in establishing a new order of God's Kingdom. Recognizing the seasons, I was sent to you as a Prophet, a forerunner of your times. The tent meetings were the birthing grounds into the establishment of faith. We experienced the uncommon anointing that has activated so many into their place of destiny. For this I am grateful. The will of God was fulfilled.

To First Baptist Church South Portsmouth, Virginia, you are my beginnings. It was there I received my first baptism by Pastor James Wynn. The disciplines of honor and respect were woven into my fabric. I was nourished in love by so many of the Elders some who still remain in faith. Thank you. My gratitude to Pastor Warren Amlet. Remember the word of prophecy and continue to respect the grace. A breath of freshness is brewing in the atmosphere; vision will come that will alter your path. Remember, "When it's time to come together, be together". Unity is the power of one embracing the trust of God's provisions. There is much to be said that this book can not contain concerning the legacy of my youth. To Rev. Womack, a brother to my father and a spiritual father to me; you have my blessings for your seeds of love you sowed into my life when I was searching in the dark trying to discover the light.

To Prophet Susan Chapman who shared with me the synergy of vision that flows from the gift of God's grace and her reckless abandonment pursuing things of the Kingdom. For your labor of love, great is your reward. To all members of the Body of Christ, my gratitude for your participation bringing reconciliation into my life., the late Mother Audrey Dockery, Pastors John and Leatha Hardy, Bishop Rodney Walker, Prophet Lynwood and Monica Cannon, and to my friends who never gave up on me and respected the word in the mouth of this Prophet, Pastors Lexta and Barbara Taylor. To my dear friend, the late Arnetta Dixon who fed me when I was hungry and loved me out of my captivity, thank you. To all the Saints in Ghana, much thanks.

To my spiritual daughter Glinda Anderson, thank you for your love and belief in me through the thick and thin. I am ever grateful for allowing me to be a voice into your life.

To my Aunt Kate, the Mother of Zion, who encouraged me to fulfill the word assigned to me for Africa. She warned me not to give hope to a suffering generation and leave them as so many that has traveled before me.

To my Aunt Annie Mae who never judged me but always showed her love even until this day. Prayers to my Aunt Thelma who I love dearly. To my oldest aunt, Aunt Pearl, thank you for your words of wisdom. I am reminded of the day you said to me when I asked you why you were reading the Enquirer Magazine. You said *"you can always find a diamond in the rough"*!

To my Mother-in-law; Mother Edna Anderson, I am grateful for allowing me the privilege to share your life and the life of your daughter. You have given me a gift. I remember when we got married, I said you lost a daughter, but you replied, I have gained a son. Peace and happiness to your days.

To my Uncle Maxwell and Marcia, who reminds me of my Father; a man of very few words but the few are profound. Thanks for your wisdom.

To Kenny Wimbush, a spiritual soldier, my friend in battle and a true warrior in Christ. Much love, eternally.

To my children Eric and Michelle, Phina and Paul, and Bota and Turquoise, and my God-daughter Debbie and Tim, you are my inheritance. It is my prayer that God's covenant grace will sustain you in the power of His love throughout your generations. Thank you for the lessons in life that have framed my future.

To my brother Francis, I take this occasion to thank you publicly for the secret things that you have done to preserve my life. I weep when I think of all that you sacrificed for me. Thank you for your love.

To all the family, Katherine and Mr. Brooks, Joyce, Sharon, James and Joni, Angie (where's your flute), thank you for your patience as I continue to allow God to perfect His righteousness in me. My nephew Jason Pettway, *"do not neglect the gift that is in you which was given to you"*. To Fran, I'm still aspiring. Thanks to Sherelle for your expertise and counsel. Remember, like minds think alike! To Keith my beloved nephew who always showed me unconditional love and favor.

A special thanks to Gloria Dawkins (Peaches) for her faithfulness, love and ever loving friendship. Eternally!

To Kernal and Marsha; my eternal friends and all of my faithful in-laws Leon and Willie, Walter and Jessie, and The Preacher anointed with grace, Rena Anderson.

To Genesis; keep the faith and cherish the mantle. The trials of life are only stepping stones for a greater future.

To Olivia; May grace, peace and mercy lightened your days. Thank you for the gift, I will never forget.

To my wife, Pastor Mary Wingate, thank you for your time, patience, love and grace as we pursue the destiny of God upon our lives. God is not through with us yet!

Kofi's Prayer

"Let the words of my mouth and the meditation of my heart, be acceptable in thy sight. Lord you are my strength and my redeemer."

Introduction

Kofi's View

Repent therefore and be converted, that your sins may be blotted out, so that "times of refreshing" may come from the "presence of the Lord", and that He may send Jesus Christ, who was preached to you before, whom heaven must receive until the "times of restoration" of all things, which God has spoken by the mouth of all his holy prophets since the world began.

Acts 3:19-21

KOFI'S VIEW

"Swimming in the Deep"

W hat a fascinating world we are living in! These are great times to be alive to witness the proliferation of change that is happening in our day. Did you know there was a new sun discovered in the distant corridor of our universe? Scientists have revealed that it is one billion times larger than our sun. It was there all this time, but we could not see it. Just because you could not see it does not negate the fact that it existed. If you can not see it, then it is invisible to you.

The depth of the universe has no boundaries, not even time which exist in the infinity of Our Creator. Nothing can escape it, not even our thoughts. Our experiences are being captured and stored in the capsule of time. Our thoughts are no more than fragments of energy collected together to give frame to an image. That is how we think. We do not think in words but in the collected energy revealed as pictures. Pictures have power. They are the parables of life.

Our words are revelation of things that we hear that translates into things that we can see.

When we speak, we produce a life in pictures to the hearing ear. The outer ear collects the energy of our words. The inner ear vibrates discriminating against interference to eliminate the unwanted gossip of words. It operates as a filter. Then, it is amplified with clarity to our minds eye to create an image. The images created in our mind are the pictures of life. Whatever a man thinketh will be reproduced in his actions. The repetitions of his actions formed from the patterns in his mind will shape the character of his heart and define the integrity in his walk.

Little Fishes

Have you ever had an ear infection? What did it sound like? If you did as I have, it sounded like your ear was filled with water, with little fishes swimming around. The little fishes are invading words that cause our hearing to become unstable. They create waves of motion bombarding the drum in our inner ear affecting our spiritual equilibrium. As they enter the cavity of our mind, they feed upon our food for thought which is the bread of life. When our mind is deprived of the budding seeds of righteousness, we become unstable in our thoughts with no clarity of the clouded patterns in our mind. The word of God is purposed to frame our perception that we may know wisdom and instruction. *"Only when we remove the intrusions from our mind will our thoughts reshape with clarity the true reflections of the pattern of our destiny."*

Speaking of fishes; there is a distinct difference between the eyes of a fish and our human eyes. A fish's eyes can discriminate in the murk and muddiness of the deep because their eyes are made larger than ours. We do not need large eyes to see, we have ears; fish don't. The most significant difference between our eyes and theirs; fish don't blink! We can blink and refresh the images of our mind. When we blink, it is an indication that our thoughts are being renewed and the images of our mind are being transformed. Every blink marks the entrance of a new revelation. It is a discovery of newly found grace waiting for our embracing. We are not controlled by the things that we see; *"we can change the things that we see"*. Just blink! In the time that it takes you to blink, you will have heard something different to see. We have no sight to see without the hearing of words that are endowed with energy to bring revelation to our sight. The entrance of God's Words gives light and understanding to the simple.

Let There Be Light

> *In the beginning God created the heavens and the earth. ²The earth was without form, and void; and darkness was on the face of the deep. And the Spirit of God was hovering over the face of the waters. ³Then God **said**, "Let there be light"; and there was light.* **Genesis 1:1-3**

"Let there be light." Light is a manifestation of something that God said. It is the result of a word spoken from His mouth that possessed the power to reveal all seen things. He separated the light from the darkness revealing ONLY

19

those things He opened our eyes to see. What He left in darkness remains hidden, yet still contains the life to produce whatever He says. Revelation comes from hidden places that have not yet had the light of discovery to shine upon it. There are things that have been here from the beginning which are now being discovered by the light of revelation. The light that shined upon the face of the deep (hidden places) and the Spirit of God that hovered over the waters of life (revealed places) created life from the incubation of time and destiny.

As the Spirit broods upon the destiny of our lives, the light of God's revelation will manifest. The illuminating light of His Spirit descends from heaven as fire burning through the barriers of darkness to bring discovery of His will. The waters above and the waters below have retreated in the presence of His firmament creating a vacuum for our habitation. We all have a signature of destiny spoken from time beginning of our place and purpose between the division of waters. As the waters from below gathered themselves into one place, the dry land called earth appeared. It had a time stamp in future times of destruction by fire. Just as the retreated waters below gathered into one place and the earth was formed, there is a promise of a new earth being made ready from the waters that remain above. It is a place of promise for the obedient of faith that have fulfilled the call of righteousness.

We were drawn from the dust of God's creation, meshed together with the dew of life as clay in the hands of a potter and flesh emerged into the image of our lives. Flesh born out of the earth remains dust until God breathes His life into us. The power of His Spirit transformed us and we became a living soul to testify of His Omnipotence. It was then we became the object of His creativity. In the inner conscience of our soul, He established His dominion. He spoke beyond the barrier of the firmament from a place of spirit and instructed us through the abilities of His Spirit to perform His word according to His plan. With power and authority, He blessed our lives with fruitfulness to recreate His image in His likeness.

He walked with us through the journey of life ultimately to reclaim that which was given to us. With our crown of fruit adorned as testimony of our obedience, we will enter into His rest with the rewards of our faith. The return of life must be greater than the value of life that was given at our conception. He commanded us to *"be fruitful and multiply"*, increase the value of our gift purposed for humanity.

The proven wisdom of life reveals that there is nothing new under the sun; just a recycling of faith from one generation to the next to produce a greater faith. The finality of faith is love as it was in the beginning so shall it endure until the end. God is the author of all creativity and is creating an eternal habitation as a reward for the obedient of faith. The foundation of His faithfulness is anchored in love which is the ultimate sacrifice one can give in exchange for a shared life unified in the power of togetherness.

The key principle to ascertain the revelations of this book, as we journey into an expansion beyond the veil of hidden things is to remember that God speaks in time and seasons of our lives. He ushers in His revelations through the *"prophetic eyes of the prophet"*. The words in the mouth of a prophet are instruments of His creativity. The Old Testament prophets walked humbly before God and knew the proven power of His words. When Elijah prayed and commanded no dew or rain, there was a performance of God's creative power that manifested.

> *Elijah was a man with a nature like ours and he prayed earnestly that it would not rain; and it did not rain on the land for three years and six months.* **James 5:17**

As we stand with God, He will do things on our behalf that we have no power to do for ourselves. When we are in communion and fellowship in the Spirit, only then can we speak accurately of His revelations. When we pray in earnest as Elijah, it is an indication of heart felt passion that we as Believers should apply to all life circumstances. It is then that our prayer life will reveal a profound level of fellowship that gives voice to the Spirit of God. Pray in earnest without ceasing until the gates of heaven are opened. The Spirit of Christ is waiting to reveal Himself with wisdom, power and authority at our awakening.

> *Now faith is the substance of things hoped for, the evidence of things not seen. ²For by it the elders obtained a good testimony. ³By faith we understand that the worlds were framed by the word of God, so that the things which are seen were not made of things which are visible.* **Hebrews 11:1-3**

Chapter 1

 A New Season

To everything there is a season, A time for every purpose under heaven.

Ecclesiastes 3:1

Have you noticed how an artist paints? He becomes very involved translating details of individual colors of patterns reflected as an image in his mind. Occasionally, he will take a step back as he struggles to translate his inner thoughts, to get a glimpse of how evolving the shape and form are coming together. If there is something that is not indicative of what he envisions, he makes the necessary corrections before bringing together the final picture. Sometimes, it is best to get an outside view to gain a full perspective. Africa was that place for me; on the outside of America looking from afar at the evolving patterns that are shaping the future of our generation.

When I look around the spiritual landscape, evidence points to a Church that is in compromise. We have been operating in the acceptance of our passivity oblivious to the changing of a new season. Compromise literally means *a reduction in the quality, value, or degree of something*. An indictment of compromise may be shocking to some and you may not agree. As you inventory your spiritual warehouse, you may conclude that you are far removed from such a bold accusation. Many of our churches have become pleasure centers; centers of convenience fulfilling the desires of men. You may have large cathedrals with chandeliers dangling in exhibition; pews made of the finest wood. You may also have the latest technology displaying on big screens the choreography of your praises; banners, flags, dancers moving in sync to the beat of your rhythm. Is it to get God's attention or the attention of your accomplishments? The faded glory of the House of Solomon arrayed in all its splendor is a beaten path of pursuit for many of our leaders who have manipulated the principles of faith for their own aspirations.

If your faith has been contaminated by the distractions of materiality, your spiritual introspection will reveal a wavering to the true cause of faith, inconsistent with God's plan for His Kingdom. You might want to consider cleaning your clock and make the necessary adjustments we so desperately need in this hour. It is through His grace that He has chosen to alter the path of our destiny. His judging eyes will always reveal the true state of our condition and render solutions to correct our course. God knows the plan He has for His Kingdom and the time and season to unveil the directions necessary to achieve His vision. Wherever He sends His Word, you will find the anointing to perform in the time that He has chosen. Our faith should be actualized to pursue those things that are before us and not the things on the beaten path, the trod path where others have already been. Yesterday was history, a place separated for learning. The opportunity for the experience of faith to intercept our gifts can only be encountered experientially.

There is a time and season for all things. It is now time to take what we have been learning and connect our faith to God's destiny purposed for our future. The obsession with learning (itching ears) without the experience of faith and an encounter with the Holy Spirit to give guidance to our visions, we are left to wander in a path where others have trod before. History has limited power of reflecting past testimonies that can't be altered but it is a true servant to gaining wisdom and understanding of the testimonies of old. The testimonies indicate where we have been but not where we are going. It does not take faith to believe what was; just accept the truth and history will become self revealing. We are generation builders. To choose not to move forward is a choice that will limit our generations to the accomplishments of our past. We are losing the battle for their future to a materialistic society of wealth and prosperity without a need for an anchor in faith.

Complacency is a process that does not happen over-night. Just as the transition of light at the twilight of morning finds us slumbering, complacency does not come upon us suddenly. After the leisure of our awakening, the comforts of life will cast a diminishing light upon our faith with no need to search for grace. At the conclusion of our day with our faith untested, complacency settles in, power-less to defend in the midst of our battles.

Observation is an element of complacency. Without the power of discernment to interact with our faith, observation will remain a risk that does not reflect in truth. We can easily get lost observing things only to be left with the distractions of our sight. It is very easy to identify a problem but the solutions require the extrapolation of our faith. Without discernment, it is possible to be in the midst of a process and not have recognition of the season you are in. This is where we find ourselves today; complacency.

Have you ever been in a hurricane? There is an eye in the center of the storm which is always peaceful and calm with no impending danger around. You can not see the storm, but you are in it. Complacency will set in and you will not have the ability to discern the sustaining grace that surrounds you. The grace is God's grace and He brings mercy and kindness in the midst of all our battles. Sometimes we forget amidst our comforts that He is in the center of our faith working things out for our good.

The Body of Christ is currently in the midst of a storm and the world around us is reflective of a body that is out of order. The silent winds of comfort have veered us off course into the tropics of man's delight. The first wave has passed by and was not purposed to wipe us out but to bring correction. We survived the long suffering of God's grace, not recognizing that the latter turbulence will come with greater intensity. If we are not vigilant, complacency will find us ill-prepared for the changing winds that await us.

There is a dangerous consequence of taking the grace of God for granted with the assumption that the sufficiency of His grace in times past is enough for our future. In our contentment, we will become vulnerable to the forces around us. Our sight will become blurred and our ability to recognize pending danger will become oblivious to us.

Rise up, you women who are at ease, Hear my voice; You complacent daughters, Give ear to my speech. ¹⁰In a year and some days You will be troubled, you complacent women; For the vintage will fail, The gathering will not come. **Isaiah 9:9-10**

Yet they would not listen to their judges, but they played the harlot with other gods, and bowed down to them. They turned quickly from the way in which their fathers walked, in obeying the commandments of the LORD; they did not do so. **Judges 2:17**

Evidence of our complacency is demonstrated by an inability to *"listen and hear"* the voice of God's authority. God's talking but we are not listening. Notice the scripture *says "they quickly turned from the way"*. My mother told me some years ago that the Church has become such a noisy place drowning out the voice of God's stillness. The vacuum created for God's habitation is flooded with the voices of men. I will admit; I have seen the circus atmosphere at the eleven o'clock hour.

Tremble, you women who are at ease; Be troubled, you complacent ones; Strip your-selves, make yourselves bare, And gird sackcloth on your waists. **Isaiah <u>9:11</u>**

Isaiah 9:11 is a prophecy to us. Prophetically speaking, our country was attacked in our complacency on 9/11. Were we quick to hear or did we continue on without resolving the true cause of our fears? Did the masking of our faith remain buried beneath the provisions of our complacency?

A New Season

It may come to you as a surprise that I separate the name *"Christian"* from that of being a *"Believer"*. While in Africa, I surveyed the terrain to discover that religion had taken a stronghold. Every denomination known by man is represented. To make things more conflicting, the people still hold on to their traditional beliefs while at the same time practicing Christianity. It is no different than here in our country where we embrace Christianity yet still hold to our belief and trust in *"capitalism, the almighty dollar"*. We can not be a servant of mammon and serve God without a conflicting interest. There are some things we desire to do for ourselves more than our commitment to the Kingdom.

I have pondered over the ministry of Evangelist Billy Graham and concluded he had a singleness of vision and purpose. For every new thing that was going on around him, he remained true to the call of faith. There was no variance in his mantle. It is so easy to abandon our vision if we are not faithfully rooted in the principles of faith amidst the seemingly success of those around us. What God has purposed for your life has a unique identifier with a spiritual earmark of grace for your success.

I came to the perception that the name Christian has become generic, identified as anyone's faith. In our culture today, everyone lay claim to the title of Christian. I heard a preacher who said *"there are many fake $20 bills, but it is not going to stop me from using mine"*. We are not to stop the things that have gotten us to where we are. The testimonies are valid and should be the foundation of our faith. Despite the counterfeits, righteousness will always prevail. We must not retreat from the foundational principles that are re-flected in truth. There is a discernable difference between those who profess Christianity and those who live the life of a Believer. Righteousness is an indication of our commit-ment to a life of obedience to the principles of faith.

Africa has always been a spiritual birthing ground embedded with a variety of beliefs. Despite their practices of juju, voodoo, or witchcraft, they are a spiritual people. Before the times of Christ, God had a people, a spiritual people that treaded the soils of Africa. The religious spirit that first introduced denominationalism upon African soil was first rooted in Catholicism from Europe where they attempted to conquer the land to advance their empire. America, the land of the *"first"* is never to be out done. We are first in pride because of the prosperity we have enjoyed. We flooded the continent of Africa with a new style of religion, *"Colonialism"*, which means to colonize and pacify. Our best only offered a watered down version of the Gospel, a religion which had its roots closer to man than God. The revelation of Christ gives liberty in the spirit but the religion of man will keep you bound in ignorance of truth.

Denominations only serve as a vehicle to keep the Body of Christ divided. How successful has that been! The efforts used to evangelize Africa were based on old methods; the methods of man and his wisdom that introduced confusion into a virgin territory. Man and the impure motives of his heart led a people further into bondage by exploiting the riches the land had to offer. While introducing religion, the subversive agent of capitalism became an ally employing methods far removed from the compassion of Christ. It is easy to see in Africa the residual of Colonialism that has left its imprint on a hurting and crying generation.

I experienced religion as a child. It became a prophet to me, leading me with a thirst for something greater than my ability to master. Afterwards, I discovered a freedom through the power of the Holy Spirit resonating in the cavity of my inner man that took absolute control of my life. It is a power that continues to sustain me in the Grace of God and keeps me separated from the powers of man.

My introduction into ministry was during the era of the *"name it claim it generation"*. Some of you are still there, resting at the place of my beginnings; *"still laying by the spring fed pool of Bethesda"*.

> *In these lay a great multitude of sick people, blind, lame, paralyzed, waiting for the moving of the water. ⁴For an angel went down at a certain time into the pool and stirred up the water; then whoever stepped in first, after the stirring of the water, was made well of whatever disease he had.* **John 5:3-4**

Laying, waiting! How powerless has the Church become, waiting for a season of revival by the Angel of God to come down. I pray that we are far removed from the expectation of God to perform something for us that He has given us power to do for ourselves. We are angels of light; the salt of the earth and the royalty of the Kingdom. There yet remain those who can still stir up the movement of the waters! Bring me the sick, blind, lame and the paralyzed and I will bring you to the angel of my faith. *"God's power has an ability to reach you beyond your limitations of reaching Him."* He will touch your life at the utterance of your cry.

We must advance beyond the dependency on man to do for us what faith is purposed to do. Faith says *"if I could just touch the hem of His garment I will be made whole".* We as believers are wearing the garment of His resurrection. It has power to heal, deliver and set the captive free. The anointing is not limited to time or seasons. The dispensation of faith ushered in by the power of God's anointing is forever present maintaining a constant flow of the living waters that brings life and healing to all of His humanity.

Grasping for the Wind

I did not realize the consequence the things I held claim to during the *"name it claim it"* era would vanish away. It had no root within itself.

> *Whatever my eyes desired I did not keep from them. I did not withhold my heart from any pleasure, For my heart rejoiced in all my labor; And this was my reward from all my labor. 11Then I looked on all the works that my hands had done and on the labor in which I had toiled; And indeed all was vanity and grasping for the wind. There was no profit under the sun.* **Ecc. 2:10-11**

Some years ago, I attended a church conference in Washington, D.C. where I was honored to hear the late Kenneth Hagin deliver a message from the Lord. His words were stunning and quite sobering. In the presence of the "who's who" that were in attendance, he said quite plainly *"this season is over"*. The era of entitlement had ended. He announced that God had shifted His empowerment from the *"Word Movement"* to that of *"Full Body Ministry"*. He gave a warning to us not to duplicate any longer the word that he had walked in for so many years that defined his ministry. But yet, many continued on with their programs without the anointing.

I admit, it can be very challenging and difficult to give up something that you have worked so hard to perfect. We are to be reminded; *"the motivation that comes from our inner life must never become secondary to the works of our hands"*. The spiritual component that defines us should always indicate a performance and pursuit for the love of God and His specific plan for our destiny.

> *For God is not unjust to forget your work and labor of love which you have shown toward His name, in that you have ministered to the saints, and do minister.*
> **Hebrews 6:10**

When ministry becomes more about you rather than what God called you to do, you will become a prime candidate for the "spirit of pride" to establish a stronghold. Failure to recognize the movement of the *"Ark of God"* will leave you in a diminished spiritual state not knowing that the *"glory of the Lord has departed"*. That is what I call the Ichabod Syndrome. We have to be very careful that we move when God moves unless we risk the chance of operating in our flesh. The Spirit of the Lord says *"I could have come and gone and you would not even have known it"*. Disobedience to the Word of God in things pertaining to His Kingdom will lead to a false sense of security established as pride. Pride always pursues a path of its own which only leads to defeat.

The Word Movement

The Word Movement was so infectious that Word Churches sprouted up all across the country. It was a movement that took us from the thirst of still waters to the shores of the living waters of faith. That season has now come to an end. We must now drink the water; replenish the spirit of man and move with the cloud of God's destiny.

The anointing for the Word Movement has been shifted into a fuller display of God's glory activating all the ministry gifting and callings the Body of Christ possesses. Previously, our focus had been looking at the elevation of the pulpits before us of men and their talents where we saw misappropriations and abuse of the gifts. We neglected the principle; *"wherever God sends His Word, He sends His abilities to perform the works of destiny".* A new season has been ushered in. It is a season of awakening to the creative power of the Spirit for the *"performance of faith".*

Much has been taught concerning tithing and giving which I believe we all should do but not enough on communion and our inner fellowship with our Father. I can not number the times I have attended services where the message was only about money; preachers twisting the revelation of God for the sake of filthy lucre. The financial interest of our churches has become a center of investment into itself; the outer house rather than investing in God's vision for the advancing of His Kingdom. This clearly indicates man's attempt to do things out of his own energy.

As I look around the landscape, I see churches on every corner without a defining mission other than to serve themselves. They house the energy of God's anointing that is purposed to bring the revelation of Jesus into our times. The revealing light of God's candle that is meant for the world to see remains hidden behind the walls of their gathering. We must remember, *"Whatever God visions, He will make provision"*.

> Unless the LORD builds the house, they labor in vain who build it; Unless the LORD guards the city, The watchman stays awake in vain. **Psalms 127:1**

It is vanity to delegate the strength of your hands to build something if God has not given you the appropriations of His vision. Despite your successes, it does not indicate the signature of His approval. There is a difference between a good thing and the right thing. A good thing is an indication that you have gone the way of the beaten path where other men have trod before but not necessarily in step on the right path to establish the legitimacy of what He has commissioned you to do. You could very well end up in error pursuing the good of your intentions rather than apprehending God's will for the sake of righteousness.

Righteousness is an indication that our character, integrity and our motives are in right standing with Him. The Spirit of God will judge our hearts and bring exposure if we are not quick to listen. The consequence can be embarrassing; *"He will lift your skirt for the world to see"*. What is hidden in the dark shall soon be brought to light. The rising of the sun does not come upon us suddenly. Transitioning from the veil of secrecy that darkness perpetuates requires time for light to emerge exposing what is buried beneath the surface of our deception.

> *Because the sentence against an evil work is not executed speedily, therefore the heart of the sons of men is fully set in them to do evil.* **Ecclesiastes 8:11**

Some of the teachings on spiritual authority were manipulated to keep the church in bondage as a servant to the desires of men. They were successful. They kept you seated in your pew and you are still sitting. Controlling spirits; men owning men! Jesus rejected the premise of the celebrity syndrome. When they tried to make him king, what was his response? He disappeared! Maybe, some of the pastors who have adapted the principle of franchising (monkey see, monkey do) should do the same; disappear! Or is the passion of your ambition resolute?

Pride and Secularism

> *Everyone proud in heart is an abomination to the LORD; Though they join forces, none will go unpunished.* **Proverbs 16:5**

I can not emphasize this enough; there is a dire consequence of entering into a spiritual agreement with the forces that perpetuate the symbols of righteousness while at the same time denying the authority and rule of the Holy Spirit. It only produces pride. Pride is the result of a lost battle of the God's Spirit taking control of our lives. When our hearts are yielded in darkness, we lose our connection to the guiding light that is purposed to lead us to the place of truth. There will always be competing forces battling for supremacy for the heart of man; the will of God versus the unyielding spirit of man. Our victories are won when our hearts are submitted and our authority relinquished to the rulership of the Holy Spirit. If man's will succeeds, *"the pride of this life, the lust of the eye and the lust of the flesh"* will defeat his purpose and those connected to his destiny.

Secularism has entered our ranks paving the way for *"spiritual capitalism"*. Perverting the spiritual jewels has only turned them into a spiritual commodity. There is a danger of our spiritual gifts being traded and even forfeited for the sake of greed which suffocates the life of integrity from a man's heart. A commodity is a *"good"* for which there is a *"demand"* exchanged for *"money"*. Some of our churches have devised spiritual schemes promoting the commodities of prophets, preachers, evangelists and teachers who are gifted and talented to perfect their schemes of exploitation. They speak with silvery tongues seasoned in deception and the pride of their elevation.

The exploitive actions of man have been escalating beyond restraint. A congregation of Believers should not be bound to the interest of any leader to keep their cash flow intact. An LLC will never give immunity from the hand of God's righteousness. The attitude of man suggests that *"as long as we fill our houses with commodities to satisfy our demand, our righteousness will prevail"*. We, the Believers are just as much to blame as the powers that harbor this level of treachery and irresponsibility. I can identify with Solomon when he said; *"I went down to the valley of nuts"*.

Have you gone nuts? What is the motivation driving your performance? What has happened to the compassion of Christ purposed for the hurting and needy?

When we, *"the Believer"*, get sick and tired of being exploited, manipulated, and used for the sake of man and his kingdom, the justice of judgment will be rendered. The light of the Holy Spirit must reach deep within the recesses of man's scaled and calloused heart to effectuate change. Even then, the struggle in the valley of our decisions will continue. It is a dangerous thing to have the body police itself using its own standards of righteousness. There has to be a voice of reason that is willing to stand and declare the righteousness of the Kingdom.

Where is the Church

> *On the following day, when the people who were standing on the other side of the sea saw that there was no other boat there, except that one which His disciples had entered, and that Jesus had not entered the boat with His disciples, but His disciples had gone away alone* [23]*however, other boats came from Tiberias, near the place where they ate bread after the Lord had given thanks* [24]*when the people therefore saw that Jesus was not there, nor His disciples, they also got into boats and came to Capernaum, seeking Jesus.*
> **John 6:22-24**

People who sometimes seek a previous move of God will often return to the place where they first received an encounter with Him. The Spirit of God is dynamic, constantly changing His performance to impact the lives of His people. The only instrument between Jesus and the world He is reclaiming are His disciples. We are the salt of the earth. If the world does not see us then how will they hear? There are times that the world seeks out the Church for answers to life's circumstances and the Church is no where to be found. They are looking for Jesus through you! They can readily identify when He is not in your camp and will seek Him out until they find Him. Scripture says that the disciples had *"gone away alone"*.

What a tragic scenario. We should never attempt to embark without the guidance and direction of the Holy Spirit. *"He will lead you and guide you into all truth."* If He is not leading you, be careful that you are not being guided by false influence into the success of failure. Failure does have power to succeed and give a false sense of accomplishments. If we do not have spiritual eyes of discernment, we, the *"Elect"* can easily be deceived.

One of my spiritual teachers taught me an important lesson; *"deliver yourself from the power and expectations of people"*. They can be an impediment to your vision.

> *Deliver yourself like a gazelle from the hand of the hunter, And like a bird from the hand of the fowler.* **Proverbs 6:5**

The devil is defeated and has a determined end. I do not give of my energy to fight a battle I know I have won. But the unpredictability of man is worrisome. Scripture says *"All the ways of man are pure in his own eyes but the Lord weighs the spirits"*. The disguised motives of man's heart lie deep within and the true value of his treasure can not be determined until revealed by the Holy Spirit. His character and integrity will reveal the level of deceit that has contaminated his heart. What proceeds from his mouth comes from the stream of the life that has been accomplished within. I have never concerned myself with merchandising the anointing that rested upon my life neither sought the approval of man. It is something I learned from the beginning which remains part of my character. I have always been the mysterious one, the renegade, The Prophet with a voice away from the beaten path. I continue marching to the beat of a different drummer.

> *Do not exalt yourself in the presence of the king, And do not stand in the place of the great; ⁷For it is better that he say to you, "Come up here," Than that you should be put lower in the presence of the prince, Whom your eyes have seen.*
> **Proverbs 25:6-7**

Our revelations should never become proprietary neither should they ever become an idol. After all, they were never ours from the beginning. Heavenly things, secret things can only be acquired through intimacy and devotion of love for our Father. As He reveals His heart in the solitude of our seeking, His grace will shower upon the just and unjust alike. His revelations should never come with a price, only the price of our obedience. God's grace is free! He advertises the truth of His Word through the life of the Believer as an indicator of the "cross" with an invitation to all mankind to accept the free-will offering of the sacrifice of Jesus.

The secret things belong to the LORD our God, but those things which are revealed belong to us and to our children forever, that we may do all the words of this law.
Deut. 29:29

But the saints of the Most High shall receive the kingdom, and possess the kingdom forever, even forever and ever.
Daniel 7:13

Revelation knowledge is the power of discovery paving the path to the fountain that reveals all life; the fountain of divine enlightenment. When we drink from that fountain, the nourishment we receive flows as a river of life with enough nutrients to continually sustain us in our journey of faith to *"work out our own salvation"*. That's something that is not left for man to do for you. They are not owners, just stewards called to protect God's investments.

But the anointing which ye have received of him abideth in you, and ye need not that any man teach you: but as the same anointing teacheth you of all things, and is truth, and is no lie, and even as it hath taught you, ye shall abide in him.
1 John 2:27

As I query the landscape, my spirit questions our motives in the application of God's Word that commands us to *"Go into all the world and preach the gospel"*. Unfortunately, man has hoarded the gifts to establish his dominion; restricting the flow of the anointing destined for a power producing generation. You only can get churched so much, and then what do you do? *"The gifts are not ours; they are assigned to our destiny."* At some point, there will be an accountability of what we have received. When the word becomes flesh, the principles of faith interacting with the power of the Holy Spirit will produce the works of obedience that proclaims God's love for His creation.

Cross Over

There are choices before us; continue in the downward spiral or join in the path to reclaim our rightful place in the Kingdom of God. At no time in our past has the power of our choices been so critical. You have heard the saying *"throw the baby out with the wash"*. Some things are good and purposed for our lives and need to be left alone. The testimonies of the elders who carved a path for our walk in faith proving the faithfulness of God's deliverance and the written word bearing proof of His truthfulness should remain as benchmarks for generations to come.

I have witnessed the mass overhaul that eliminated the testimonies of the Saints for the sake of something new that bore the resemblance of God's acceptance. There are some things that are destined to never be removed while others if not removed, will remain as a serious distraction. Peripheral distractions surfacing in the destined path of faith are a hindrance and have no part in God's plan for our lives. We must be vigilant of our time and spiritual energy. If not, we will wander in the desert of God's prophetic plan.

> *And Joshua said to them: "Cross over before the ark of the LORD your God into the midst of the Jordan, and each one of*

43

you take up a stone on his shoulder, according to the number of the tribes of the children of Israel, ⁶that this may be a sign among you when your children ask in time to come, saying, 'What do these stones mean to you?' ⁷Then you shall answer them that the waters of the Jordan were cut off before the ark of the covenant of the LORD; when it crossed over the Jordan, the waters of the Jordan were cut off. And these stones shall be for a memorial to the children of Israel forever. **Joshua 4:5-7**

"Cross Over." Take a step of faith to ensure the revelation of His promises. He will do nothing until you first get your feet wet. Remove the training wheels of your comfort and witness the performance purposed for your success. God makes covenant with us by those things that He instructs us to do. The covenant is a promise to us and future generations. We are instructed to establish and forever keep the landmarks as a testimony memorializing the omnipotence of His power and faithfulness. He always attaches His abilities to perform His Word as a testimony of grace and His never ending love. Restoration of our spiritual landmarks is a key indication that our hearts have changed and remain in pursuit of the instructions of faith.

Far be it from us that we should rebel against the LORD, and turn from following the LORD this day, to build an altar for burnt offerings, for grain offerings, or for sacrifices, besides the altar of the LORD our God which is before His tabernacle. **Joshua 22:29**

Two Dogs Don't Make it Right

> *Professing to be wise, they became fools,*
> *[23]and changed the glory of the incorruptible*
> *God into an image made like corruptible*
> *man and birds and four-footed animals*
> *and creeping things. [24]Therefore God also*
> *gave them up to uncleanness, in the lusts*
> *of their hearts, to dishonor their bodies*
> *among themselves, [25]who exchanged the*
> *truth of God for the lie, and worshiped and*
> *served the creature rather than the Creator,*
> *who is blessed forever. Amen.*
> **Romans 1:22-25**

It is considered an abomination to know God and exist in the discovery of His grace but refuse to glorify Him as The Creator. God has existed; is existing and will forever exist from eternity beginning to eternity end. The suppression of truth causes unrighteousness leading men down a dark unforgiving path of judgment and destruction. Alienated from truth can only actualize the limited power that flesh provides; *"lust"*. Lust is a pure indication that the Spirit of God is overshadowed by the desires of man in his pursuits of the lust of the flesh, lust of the eye and the pride of life. When there is no accountability of the Holy Spirit ruling within, what remains is just the shell of His occupation. When the Spirit is lifted from us, our countenance will continue to glow until the dimming light is fully extinguished. It is like the brilliance of fire so pure and vibrant; dancing, pulsating with the colors of life until the chill waters of our desire is poured upon it. What once was a fire is now reduced to a smothering of smoke.

The fire of God pulsates in the orchestrated rhythm of His Spirit bringing warmth and fuel that drives the heart of man. Located in the center of our being, it sheds light throughout the body illuminating the recesses of our conscience and igniting sparks of truth to our judgment. The fuel of fire is maintained through worship, our connection to the *"eternal flame"*. Without the fire of worship, we are lost in obscurity of simmering smoke, drowning in the sea of our own passion.

When disobedience enters, it separates us from the law of truth of *"God's Righteousness"*. Our lamp will begin to diminish due to the hardening of our heart; soon there is no light to see. The pathway of repentance still remains open, but we continue in darkness scaled by our deception. With no light to drive our conscience, we become seared in unrighteousness, alienated from truth. Our garment of purity and righteousness is exchanged from incorruptible to corruptible; from pure to uncleanness; from honor to dishonor. The only hope that remains is a vain hope in the image of the flesh, *"the creature"*. We exchanged the power of The Creator who is blessed forever for the *"lie"* of the creature professing to be wise. The heart that was filled with light and peace is now darkened, burning in lust that rules within. There is no awakening, for there is no light to see, no retention of God in their knowledge and a mind debased of truth.

Chapter 2

THE CLARION WORD

For God may speak in one way, or in another, Yet man does not perceive it. ¹⁵In a dream, in a vision of the night, When deep sleep falls upon men, While slumbering on their beds, ¹⁶Then He opens the ears of men, And seals their instruction. ¹⁷In order to turn man from his deed, And conceal pride from man.

Job 33:14-17

C larion is the voice of God. It is a prophetic word sealed with apostolic instructions. When God trumpets His Word from a prophetic stream, HE speaks within a pure stream of light which is called "clarion". It requires a prophetic ear to hear the voice that speaks with "clarion clarity". The Prophet John, exiled on the Isle of Patmos, said in the Book of Revelation *"I was in the Spirit on the Lord's Day, and I heard behind me a loud voice, as of a trumpet"*. The voice of the trumpet is the articulation of the true heart of God. In every major revelation from Him, there is a paradigm shift of moving out of one season into another dimension of prophetic truth. He always speaks through a voice of the willing that have separated themselves unto him.

> *Where there is no revelation, the people cast off restraint; But happy is he who keeps the law.* **Proverbs 29:18**

In one of my night seasons, I heard the voice of that trumpet! The Spirit of God revealed to me the image of a church being restored from its ruins to its original form. The work began from the altar to the doorway; from inside to out. After the completion of the restoration, a steeple was placed on top of the church. What followed spoke volumes into my spirit. The steeple spoke as the voice of the trumpet! I looked up and saw neon fluorescent bulbs pulsating in an array of lights in the brilliance of high definition. It revealed a glaring word that gave indication of God's prophetic intent for this season. CLARION!

The Clarion Word

"Wake up and arise! The Church has entered into a season of restoration. Restore the Body of Christ in all things according to God's prophetic blueprint."

Restoration Begins in the House of God

Before restoration can come to the Body of Christ, the visitation of the judgment of God to "destroy the works of the devil" must precede His redemptive grace.

Yet if any man suffer as a Christian, let him not be ashamed; but let him glorify God on this behalf. For the time is come that judgment must begin at the house of God: and if it first begin at us, what shall the end be of them that obey not the gospel of God? **1 Peter 4:16-17**

It is time to wake up! Arise, for the Lord has spoken. Our obedience is required to submit to the prophetic process of bringing restoration to God's true divine order; *"the Apostolic Pattern"*. The apostolic pattern is the spiritual imprint of the Body of Christ operating in the full measure of what He intended. The tabernacle paradigm of Jesus being the chief cornerstone with the foundation being built upon the mastery of the Apostles and Prophets serves as the vehicle that will facilitate the necessary change needed in order for the body to mature and fulfill the mission of establishing the Kingdom of God.

The most significant part of change is vacating the old order of government for the new. Jesus said that *"you can not put new wine into old skins"*. Renovation begins at the altar and displays outwardly what has been accomplished within. Our altars must be rebuilt upon the foundation of our beginnings; prayer! There is a dire consequence in moving forward with old methods without adapting the wisdom and instructions that God has in this hour. "A wise man will hear and increase in learning by apprehending in prayer the grace needed to fulfill God's prophetic plan."

> *No man putteth a piece of new cloth unto an old garment, for that which is put in to fill it up taketh from the garment, and the rent is made worse. Neither do men put new wine into old bottles: else the bottles break, and the wine runneth out, and the bottles perish: but they put new wine into new bottles, and both are preserved.*
> **Matthew 9:16-17**

The pride of man and his accomplishments must yield to God's government. The Body of Christ is going through the process of change that will fitly join together all of the giftings and callings of the Kingdom. The result will prove to be the greatest outpouring of our time. Change has consequences that will invoke contradictions and variance at every level. It also has the ability to sever away illegitimate connections that have attached to our destiny. Much of the energy of the Body of Christ has been misappropriated pursuing the schemes of men who have purposed in their heart to establish their name at any cost. We have entered a season where our desires must be compressed to compliance for exercising His will in our lives above our own.

Through out the ages, God has unveiled His mysteries to make known His intentions. The mysteries are often judged and filtered in the conscience of man and rendered as a denial of present day truth. Truth must be accepted and applied to bring man in right standing. *"It is our denial that hinders us the most."* When God releases a word into our dimension of time, we are challenged with obedience to fulfill His instructions. Do you remember Jonah and the instructions he received? God spoke with clarity. What was Jonah's response? He ran in the opposite direction. We, the Body of Christ are the Jonah of today headed in a backwards direction. Most assuredly, we will suffer the correction of our disobedience. After the correction of Jonah's error, he demonstrated a resilience to complete the call upon his life and fulfilled the Lord's instructions. The Body of Christ must demonstrate the power of resilience that can only be accomplished through our humility.

Resilience

Jesus is looking for resilient Believers who can bounce back and reclaim the destiny committed upon their lives. Resilient is a word that is synonymous to elasticity. It represents the property of a material that causes it to resume its original size and shape after having been compressed or stretched by an external force. That sounds like a lot of Christians I know, including myself, that have been stretched on every side. Have you ever been pressed to the point that you have said *"this gets on my nerves"?* What you have experienced is stress. Stress is an indicator of the pressings that we as Believers must endure if we are to pursue the path of perfecting our faith. The pressings that come on every side are to keep us walking the straight and narrow in pursuit of our destiny.

> *Remember the word to Your servant, Upon which You have caused me to hope. [50]This is my comfort in my affliction, For Your word has given me life.*
> **Psalms 119:49-50**

Too much stress causes structural changes and leads to a deformity referred to as strain. Strain is an indication of the struggles we face that begin to take a toll on our lives. If we are not careful, it will affect our character and bring compromise to our integrity. It is not a wise thing to ignore the weight of your afflictions and continue to carry them beyond your ability. *"There is a time to consider letting go and letting God."* You are not a super hero. There are some things developed out of our walk of faith that are purposed for a lasting testimony of our humility. The Apostle Paul had a thorn in his side that was continually with him; Jacob wrestled with an angel and was left with a limp; Jesus had the cross of Calvary ever before Him. Just as those who moved in faith, we are to take up our cross daily as a testimony of our commitment of obedience.

> *You have dealt well with Your servant, O LORD, according to Your word. ⁶⁶Teach me good judgment and knowledge, For I believe Your commandments. ⁶⁷Before I was afflicted I went astray, But now I keep Your word.* **Psalms 119:65-67**

We can invite unnecessary warfare and afflictions to come into our lives because of our disobedience. The consequences that ensue are not worth the price of discipleship. If we are wise, we will learn the lessons of affliction and be more inclined to walk the path of obedience to gain good judgment and knowledge. We have all faced the strain of our circumstances as well as those that we are carrying for others. The amount of stress and strain that we can maintain is determined by the making of our spiritual fabric. Faith, hope and charity are the spiritual jewels woven into our plate of armour ready at the summons for our defense.

> *Stand therefore, having girded your waist with truth, having put on the breastplate of righteousness, ¹⁵and having shod your feet with the preparation of the gospel of peace; ¹⁶above all, taking the shield of faith which you will be able to quench all the fiery darts of the wicked one. ¹⁷And take the*

helmet of salvation, and the sword of the Spirit, which is the word of God; [18] praying always with all prayer and supplication in the Spirit. **Ephesians 6:14-18**

What is woven into you? Do you possess the power of resilience to bounce back and resume? *"God will never put more on you than you can handle."* He knows your spiritual makeup. If we maintain the protective shield of righteousness, we will prevail through the contrary winds of time that challenge our faith.

We That are Strong

Some years ago, my Mother recognized one of the Saints in her church in spiritual distress. She was moved with compassion and did something I have never seen before. She said, *"Daughter, you can't carry this. It will defeat you. Give it to me"*. She knelt at the feet of the young lady and told her *"lay your hands on my shoulders"*. Spiritually, that was a moment in time I will never forget. A short time passed by when I received a call from my Mother. She told me that her hair was beginning to fall out and how oppressed she was feeling. I was quickened in the Spirit to remind her of what she was confronting. I reminded her of the moment when she took on the burdens which were upon the young lady. She was experiencing the weight of those oppressive spirits that were cast upon her that she invited into her warfare. With prayer and the strength of the Holy Spirit, she overcame the vexations that had clutched her spirit. I admire her much for the love that she gave in a time of someone else's need. The strength of the strong should bear the burdens of the weak, but we must be careful! When a demand is put upon the anointing that we are walking in, there has to be power to sustain. It can be tempting at times to bite off more than you can chew. Ask any child; you will choke. The anointing is corporate to all Believers of Faith and our sufferings and burdens are a shared responsibility for the sustaining of the whole.

> *Then I will come down and talk with you there. I will take of the Spirit that is upon you and will put the same upon them; and they shall bear the burden of the people with you, that you may not bear it yourself alone.* **Numbers 11:17**

As Believers, the test of our strength is weighed in the balance of our humility; *"we that are strong ought to bear the infirmities of the weak"*. This suggests there is something that we "ought" to be doing that we are not. When someone says you ought to, it is a suggestion that something is lacking in your performance. It is an indication of a weakness that has a consequential affect in someone else's life; a demand put on your anointing to effectuate life in others. The gifts are purposed for others and not ourselves. There are times our journey can be physically and spiritually challenging. Every battle is not meant for us to go through on our own. There are no super heroes left on this side of the cross of burdens. If so, I adjure you; "physician heal thyself". We are the full compliment of God's gifting incorporated with the power to administer healing and deliverance to those we encounter.

The pressure within your inner man and the daily pressings that come from the outside of your faith will affect your ability to cope. You must have the ability to adjust to any outside pressure trying to break you. You could bend and buckle under the weight without the preparation that faith produces. The faith level for one is not necessarily the same for another. We must maintain a balance between the trials we are experiencing of being tossed to and fro and the wisdom of our experiences to overcome the battles that are before us. The purpose of our trials is not to wipe us out but bring a greater anointing into our life. Our resiliency in faith should have a sling shot effect. The stretching is painful and uncomfortable but the come back is with a force of quickness and power that will knock down everything in its path. Our resilience advances us into a level of faith that is an uncommon product of our belief.

The Little Boats

> *Now when they had left the multitude, they took Him along in the boat as He was. And other little boats were also with Him.*
> **Mark 4:36**

It is not all the time that we have strength and the ability to do things on our own without the help of others. We all have spiritual and physical limitations. Notice that the scripture says *"they took Him as He was"*. God will join those to you who are entrusted to your destiny. Regardless of the venue, they are assigned to provide gifting for your success. Spiritual recognition is vital to determine who is sent to you. Despite the size of the *"little boats"*, never discount the value of those that are there to help you. Regardless of the insignificance you may attach to their ministry, they are purposed for your destiny. In my early years, I was given a prophecy for an established national prophet. He rejected my attempt to speak the word that the Lord had given me for him. I was in a little boat, drove a little car, my name was not in lights and had no status as a national prophet. How ridiculous it is to believe because you do not have an established name, the voice of God is mute. God chooses to use whoever he desires. The responsibility is ours to hear and spiritually discern whether it be of the Spirit. It is very dangerous to appoint your own prophet and rely exclusively on that voice to be the voice of the Spirit. Moses is dead! The days of a king and his prophet are yesterday's revelation. We, the Body of Christ are the prophetic voice of the Kingdom authorized as agents of Jesus Christ to wear His prophetic mantle. In His dominion, we rule under the government of His Spirit. We are all called as ministers of reconciliation anointed to preach, heal the broken hearted and set the captives free.

> *The lambs will provide your clothing, And the goats the price of a field; 27You shall have enough goats' milk for your food, For the food of your household, And the nourishment of your maidservants.*
> **Proverbs 27:26-27**

The Bible says that we are to recognize those that labor amongst us. Whatever our destiny may be, God will provide us with the gifts and provisions to accomplish our vision. The little lambs that He sends our way are there to secure our material provisions in exchange for spiritual empowerment. Keep your goats; they have a purpose! Don't run them off because of the indifference of their persuasions. Everybody connected to you does not believe as you but they are there to sustain you. They will put food on your table! It takes the wisdom of the Spirit to differentiate truth from one's own righteousness. Be careful; some of those that are sent to you as a servant, you will end up serving them. The last and the least amongst you who are humbled in spirit will be exalted in due season.

Many are the Afflictions

There is a consistent pattern in scripture that reveals whenever the Body of Christ is strengthen and multiplying greatly, a subsequent warfare is evident. At the time that Moses came along, Israel had increased in abundance and became exceedingly mighty. Israel became a threat to Pharaoh and he began to bring affliction upon them. But scripture says that Israel was resilient. *"The more they were afflicted, the more they multiplied and grew."* If the enemy to your destiny is determined to stop you, he will devise a plan by any means necessary to defeat you, including the death of your generation. Pharaoh proceeded with a plan to kill every male child born to the Israelites. Moses' parents hid him until the child grew to the point that they could not hide him any longer. They made him an ark and sent him down the river.

Moses' sister stood on the banks of the river to watch and to know what would become of the child. God had an angel watching to protect him and He has an angel assigned to your destiny. Just as the parents of Moses, some of the problems that we are holding on to need to be separated from us. We need to release them into trusting hands and believe *"what God has promised, he is faithful to perform it, even to the fulfilling of His word"*. God's got a solution for you. He has already planned your success. Regardless of our battles, *"many are the afflictions of the righteous but God will deliver us out of them all"*.

The enemy will never quit! Scripture says the devil left Jesus for a season for a more opportune time. When Moses and the children of Israel were crossing the divided waters of the Red Sea, Pharaoh didn't quit. He pursued them and the sea closed in and drowned him and his army! We can not walk in a deliverance that does not have our name assigned to it. Come to know God for yourself. What He meant for you doesn't mean it will work for someone else.

There are times the decisions that we need to make will be of benefit to all that are connected to our destiny. In our efforts to please God, He will interact with our faith if we would only trust Him. Through faith, the discovery of His grace will be sufficient for all life's circumstances.

> *It is time for You to act, O LORD, For they have regarded Your law as void. Therefore I love Your commandments More than gold, yes, than fine gold! Therefore all Your precepts concerning all things consider to be right; I hate every false way. Your testimonies are wonderful; Therefore my soul keeps them. The entrance of Your words gives light; It gives understanding to the simple.* **Ps. 119:126-130**

Chapter 3

The Secret Place

He who dwells in the secret place of the Most High Shall abide under the shadow of the Almighty. ²I will say of the LORD, "He is my refuge and my fortress; My God, in Him I will trust." ³Surely He shall deliver you from the snare of the fowler And from the perilous pestilence. ⁴He shall cover you with His feathers, And under His wings you shall take refuge; His truth shall be your shield and buckler. **Psalms 91:1-4**

Have you ever taken a refresher course? If your answer is yes, it is refreshing to know that you were seeking knowledge of things learned in times past. It only was a reminder of what to, how to, where to and when to. The purpose of a refresher is to activate and repair the disconnection of knowledge from yesterday's past in preparation for what exists tomorrow. If we are able to bridge the gap between now and then, we will arrive at that place called restoration; *the ordering of things in its rightful place*. As Believers, we must have a respect and knowledge of God's order. The lack of that knowledge will result in the body operating in a weaker state only to produce division; a separation of our life from His life.

The prophetic principles implemented in God's pattern of the Tabernacle are essential to our faith. The Tabernacle the Lord revealed to Moses had three major progressions; "the outer court, the inner court, and the sanctuary of God's habitation, the Most Holy Place".

I Saw the Light

For years, I stood on the peripheral of God's Kingdom, watching from the outside with curiosity. I took note of the lives of those who had forsaken all and denied the natural world access for an unseen force that was beyond my recognition. I noticed they were being guided by an invisible force and speaking uncommon words from another dimension of existence. I saw the performance of powers that witnessed to me; opening blind eyes and deaf ears, the sick getting healed. It became a provocation to me, challenging the foundation of all that I believed. I discovered that there was a deeper power with the ability to see things in the dark more than I could recognize in the light.

As a soldier in Vietnam, an unwilling child launched into the turmoil of war, I searched for this light to bring healing to my soul in the midst of hostilities, death and the daily confrontation of overwhelming fear. I was surrounded by God's grace which should have been sufficient, but I failed to recognize it. I wandered endlessly looking for something to attach my hope to but still could not see the *Hope of Ages* that was sustaining me. The forever presence of God was all around me but I was blinded by my fears. I was defeated; trapped inside of a conscience that would not release me.

In the process of searching through the entanglement of my spirit, a word of hope connected to the anguish of my seeking. It was the voice of my Mother; the voice of love that never abandoned me. She said, *"Son, come home"*. The disappointments of my father in my quandary loomed in my memory. As I struggled to get free from the connected web of confusion that had me bound, the words of my father's song began singing in my ear; *"There is a bright side somewhere, don't you rest until you find it, there is a bright side somewhere".* The song continued resonating within and would not stop; *"I will go into my secret closet and I will fall down on my knees".* With a weeping spirit, I found the passion for tears. I became humbled and bowed down on bended knee. Suddenly, the healing of tears flooded the chambers of my heart. The condemnation lifted from my conscience. I was being made whole again. I was ushered into that place of surrender; no more heartache; no more pain and suffering; no more frustration and confusion; no more weeping.

The power to weep had left me; buried in the sea of forgetfulness. I was free! Free from the condemnation that had clutched my spirit. Free to reclaim life and believe again. On bended knee, I cried with a loud voice, *"Lord, open my eyes that I may see; open my ears that I may hear, loose my tongue that I may speak".* Suddenly, I could hear with clarity and my eyes opened to truth. I began to hear voices from afar calling me. I looked up and saw that the heavens were opened. Then a thundering voice from above spoke and the earth began to shake. The tombstone of defeat planted on my destiny was shattered into pieces and with a shout, the voice from above said *"loose him".* The keys to my captivity that had shackled my mind, soul and body released me from the valley of despair into the flourishing pastures of the newness of life.

The gravitational powers that held me earthbound responded in kind and released their hold on me. I was drawn upward, accelerating into a higher dimension. I was learning to fly again. Not bound by the captivity of the world any longer, I began to soar in the presence of God far above any heights I had ever attained. The wind of His Spirit embraced me and thrust me even higher. I crossed the barriers of time and seasons finally arriving in a world full of love and peace.

With gates of pearls and floors mirrored in gold, the strings of my heart began to play as the angels joined in a symphony of praise. Heaven's choir began to sing "Sweet Lamb of God" at the sight of His Rod. I saw my Mother shouting with joy with a crown on her head that was minus one star. Deep within, with my soul overwhelmed with ponder to the weepings of my spirit, I knew then I was the vacant star missing from her crown. In the blink of an eye, the Spirit escorted me to a chair where I was seated beside the Chair called Righteousness. A scroll was handed to me; I opened it and read the word; *"HOPE"*. I had encountered the Hope of Ages. I could not see His face but I felt His presence. I became weak from the power of His love that stretched endlessly throughout all eternity. I was bathed in the power of His expectation and adorned with the wings of His Spirit and realized that *"now, I can fly"*.

With the voice of His Spirit blasting in my ear as a sound of a trumpet giving summons of His power, the vision of my future was sealed in the scroll of HOPE. In a trilogy of sound as a united symphony, He echoed His command, "Return to Bethel". With majestic speed as a comet of fire, I traveled the heavens and returned with the scroll in my hand. I landed on top of a mountain; Elijah was waiting, doubled in his mantle. With an urgency, he cast His mantle upon me and said *"Not by my might, nor by my power, but by My Spirit said the Lord"*. Just as quickly as he appeared; he disappeared. It was now time to descend the mountain. With the scroll of *"HOPE"*, I now began to walk; step by step into the preparation of His grace that was waiting my obedience. Every step is a step of faith into a divine encounter only discovered by the depth of His gifting. Wherever I am sent, the scroll is opened and ready to read. For every season, God will reveal His Word.

When the scroll of life is finally finished, I will adorn my wings again and take flight. Not to the top of the mountain but from *"whence I cometh, searching for the crown with a vacant star"*. The vacant star of her crown will be filled with sparkling jewels rejoicing in His eternal light. I will take my place with the glow of angels as a twinkling star pulsating with praise of His eternal glory, waiting for the stars of my own crown to be adorned with light. Heaven is waiting for me and I cherish the hope that someday I will hear the trumpets blow. From the life of despair to the arisen height of glory, the message of the scroll gives hope to the weary; *"faint not in well doing for soon shall be your reward"*.

The Tabernacle Experience

In a vision in the night, I was in a wilderness place; a desert, somewhere secluded in time. There was a huge tent in the middle of nowhere. I went inside and was seated in the front row. In front of me, I could hear the majestic voices of angels singing praises unto God and bowing in the presence of a King. I could hear them, but I could not see their faces. I noticed all the fixtures and ornaments were made of gold. It was such a sweet aroma in the atmosphere. I looked behind me, dressed in white as far as the eye could see were multitudes of Saints. What a beholding sight! Around noon time, everyone began to leave. I asked a question; where are they going? I heard a voice that said they are going to eat. I made the motion to get up but a hand came from behind and touched my shoulder sitting me down. Then the voice said to me; *"You can't leave, you are our Priest"*. I began to feel so lonely and detached when I realized that I was never to leave the sanctuary of His Presence. Whatever was needed for my sustaining would come from inside His dwelling place.

The next morning, I awoke to my daily devotionals still remembering the vision I had during the night. I opened my Bible to eat my daily Bread. This Bible was very special to me. During the time of my restoration, a journey that took me ten years to complete from the delusions and sufferings of war to the portals of grace, I discovered a new life hidden behind the veil of words. Not long after the experience that brought a revolution into my life, I had gone to a thrift store. As a child, I would go with my Mother to thrift stores and yard sales where she would find old, neglected and left for dead doll babies that no one else wanted. She would bring them home and restore them. If they needed clothes, she would make them clothes. If they needed shoes, she would get shoes. If they were missing an eye or limb, she would find them eyes for sight and limbs to walk. She would nourish them back to life and kept them as her treasure. What I was witnessing was the performance of the power of love and the joy of redemption. We never called my Mother, Mama; we called her *"Di"*, her sisters called her *"Dolly"*. I now can see how spiritually appropriate the synergy of her name and gifts were interwoven into her destiny. What manifested out of her life was the power of God's love for all His creation. There was always a smile and the desire to serve her humanity embracing them with the love of Christ.

While at the thrift store, I noticed an old beat up tattered Bible in a trash bin. It needed a home but little did I know it would become my home. The cover was worn beyond recovery from centuries of passage waiting for my discovery. I searched until I found someone who would restore it. It became the first Bible I would own. For some reason, it meant everything to me; it was my testimony, my life story. Just as my Mother restored life to the dolls that were wounded, hurt, homeless and cast aside, the Holy Spirit was bringing restoration to my life. What was missing, I found between the pages; with no eyes to see, I found His Spirit; no feet to walk, I found my wings; no hands to build, I found my sword and shield; no ears to hear, I discovered prayer; no voice to speak, I found His Word. I found all my senses in this tattered *"Testament"*; I found my life.

It is an old Bible but it has a very good reference for the study of scripture. What was reprinted a hundred years ago had enough life reserved for my future. This particular morning as I was researching the scriptures, I happened to turn to a page that had the exact image of the tent that was in my vision. I looked closer, with excitement brewing within I discovered the word *"tabernacle"*. The revelation revealed to me in the night was now becoming clear. The mantle that is upon my life is a ministry unto Him. It is a separated life with a voice that speaks in times and seasons. It is the commissioned voice of the Prophet.

Faith comes by hearing and hearing by the word of God. After hearing the word with the quickening power of the Holy Spirit, I was confronted with choices: *"choose life and live or live the life I had chosen"*. I yielded! A new beginning had arisen, the beginnings of a life of faith. I was taken through the entry way of a newly discovered life of destiny, the Outer Court of the Kingdom of God.

The Outer Court

In the Outer Court, I discovered God's redeeming grace of salvation and the compassion of His forgiveness by surrendering my life in exchange for the unlimited power of His love. I became humbled to the death of all things around me, including the death of myself to fulfill God's destiny upon my life. I was introduced into a life of faith where I discovered the compassion that faith produces. The ultimate sacrifice of faith is the determined end of ourselves for an experience in a fuller life of purpose.

I was thrown upon the altar for the burning of my flesh. I was burned to a crisp! I felt the fire burning but it was the fire that was burning on the inside of me. My heart was being purified; my soul was being washed and cleansed. I was being validated through a process tried by fire and salted with the righteousness of God. Salt was the preservative that was missing from my life and the fire purified me and burned away the liability of my past.

The fire of God will burn away any connections to the place of our defeats by destroying the path back into darkness. It burns away anything and everything that separates our life from His. I had a made up mind! I believed the life I was living could not compare to the life that was before me. Nothing remained but His redeeming grace. Remember Lazarus who experienced the power of God's resurrection? There was still something needed to engage this new life that resurrection alone could not do. He needed deliverance! The cords of bondage needed to be severed away from his hands and feet. We can not expect God to use us, thrust into a life of faith, with our hands and feet bound to the place of our defeat. We will become spiritually handicapped with an ineffective testimony. If we do not remain in the fire long enough, we will not completely be liberated from the powers that kept us in bondage.

> *"We will burn until we are done; done with the world, done with a life of wickedness and disobedience and completely done with ourselves."*

I have seen the consequence of entering into the next level of development in the life of faith without completing the process of fire. We will carry around unnecessary baggage; the same attitudes, same behavior of the life we had wandering in the wilderness of life. God will bring deliverance if we are committed to a life dedicated unto Him. The judgment of the fire should have consumed all the old, lifeless, withered and dried up things for the creation of a new life of freedom. If we are not patient, what the fire is meant to do will only be done in part. We then become an ineffective witness; speaking words of truth with a life contrary to the testimony of the Believer.

The transforming power of God changes everything that it encounters from one nature into another. If our process is complete, He will seal us in His righteousness with the infilling of the Holy Ghost. The Holy Ghost is the promise that comes to the life of every Believer. He is the guarantee of a fuller occupation of God's glory. He possesses the power to sustain us in the grace that God has purposed for our future. He brings power to our gifts to operate in a life of faith away from the dependency of our natural talents and abilities. After the process of burning is complete, we are ready to be offered as a vessel of honor; a *"servant"* in the House of Faith, entering the hidden dimension of His grace.

> *For everyone will be seasoned with fire and every sacrifice will be seasoned with salt.*
> **Mark 9:49**

> *I beseech you therefore, brethren, by the mercies of God, that ye present your bodies a living sacrifice, holy, acceptable unto God, which is your reasonable service. 2And be not conformed to this world: but be ye transformed by the renewing of your mind, that ye may prove what is that good, and acceptable, and perfect, will of God.*
> **Romans 12:1-2**

The Inner Court

From the Outer Court, that place of surrender, we enter into the Inner Court; from the place of public consumption to a life veiled in secrecy. It is the place where our service is required for ministry for maintaining the House of God and for the edification of the Body of Christ. We are presented the keys to the Kingdom and adorned with the garments of ministry to live a life of faith dedicated to perfect the lives of the Saints. The performance of faith is a requirement of our gifts to be manifested in this new life of servanthood. We are transformed into stewards of the Kingdom. Much is entrusted to us; obedience, faithfulness, honor and most of all the transforming power of love.

We have entered into is a festival of love, fellowship and communion with one another where we become servants at the table of the righteous. We render that which has been perfected in us to establish the Body of Christ in the works of the Spirit. We become body builders to bring strength, boldness and courage to carry out the commandments of Christ to deliver the Gospel of the Kingdom of God to a world void of the seeds of righteousness. This is true *"love ministry"*; a place of equal distribution where we minister one to another perfecting the principles of love. Scripture says "how can you say you love your Father whom you have not seen and don't love your brother". There were two commandments Jesus gave that fulfilled the requirement of obedience to all the law; the love of God and the love of His humanity. Love is complete and has no boundaries. The measure of the fullness of Christ is weighed in the balance of love.

When He ascended up on high, He led captivity captive, and gave gifts unto men. Now that He ascended, what is it but that He also descended first into the lower parts of the earth? He that descended is the same also that ascended up far above all heavens, that he might fill all things. And He gave some, apostles; and some, prophets; and some, evangelists; and some, pastors and teachers; For the perfecting of the saints, for the work of the ministry, for the edifying of the body of Christ: Till we all come in the unity of the faith, and of the knowledge of the Son of God, unto a perfect man, unto the measure of the stature of the fullness of Christ. **Ephesians 4:8-13**

After the service of our ministry in the Inner Court and our obedience has been proven concerning the visible things of the Kingdom, then and only then can we begin to be perfected in the things which are part of our invisible destiny; a dimension uniquely separated from the familiarity of any past encounters.

We should no longer be children, tossed to and fro and carried about with every wind of doctrine by the trickery of men in the cunning craftiness of deceitful plotting [15]*but speaking the truth in love, may grow up in all things into Him who is the head Christ* [16]*from whom the whole body, joined and knit together by what every joint supplies, according to the effective working by which every part does its share, causes growth of the body for edifying of itself in love.* **Eph. 4:14-16**

The Secret Place

In the final dimension of God's Grace, we discovered that the veil was already rent in two from top to bottom; from heaven to earth with a newly discovered path into the hidden dimension. It ushered in a new season. The works of our hands had finished and what was left to be completed was above and beyond human intervention. It is a resting place; freed from the responsibility of duty. With no more workings of the flesh, the power of the Spirit to perform the works of faith was released. It gave us access directly to the source and released the power of grace to perfect the work of the law.

When the curtain was rent, it released the resurrection power of Jesus and the bodies of the fallen Saints came out of their graves. That power is still here today. God's Spirit is eternal and the resurrection power of Jesus remains. What happened two-thousand years ago was the first fruit of our eternal occupation in His dwelling place. The rent left an entry way into the presence of the Lord, the dwelling place of God that we call His Secret Chambers.

God's hiding place now becomes our hiding place. There we began to live under the shadow of the Most High God and receive the revelation that comes from His presence. It is only in *"This Place, His Presence"* that we experience a divine encounter and a spiritual makeover. Our lives are transformed from a world labored with the weight of visible things into a spiritual world where the invisibility of faith is governed by the rule of the Holy Spirit. Our ministry then becomes a ministry unto Him. The experience in a life of secrecy in the presence of God will always produce a performance of public power.

The secret place is a refined place cultivated out of our obedience. The price is costly and the sacrifice remains to be defined to dwell in His presence. This spiritual mandate requires an absolute surrender of our will to pursue the divine will of God. Surrender says *"it is not my will Father, but only Your will be done"*.

The Saints of the Most High, the Body of Christ are the living Tabernacle of God for the indwelling and fulfilling of His desire. Every anointing where the glory of God is manifested requires a covering.

> *He that dwells in the secret place shall abide under the shadow of the almighty. I will say to the Lord, He is my refugee and my fortress, my God in Him will I trust. Surely He shall deliver me from the snare of the fowler and from the noisome pestilence. He shall cover me with His feathers and under His wings shall I trust.*
> **Psalms 91:1-4**

> *Or do you not know that your body is the temple of the Holy Spirit who is in you, whom you have from God, and you are not your own? 20For you were bought at a price; therefore glorify God in your body and in your spirit, which are God's.*
> **1 Corinthians 6:19-20**

Fresh Oil

In the presence of God, there is nothing that separates our life from His, not even a strand of hair upon our head. Stripped to the core with my head shaven bare, the olive branch of peace adorns my crown. Bearing olives pressed out of His love, a river of oil flows upon my crown as the oil descending from Aaron's beard. He anoints my head with *"fresh oil from heaven"* filling my cup overflowing with love. I drink the wine of oil to celebrate His gift, a river of life with waters everlasting. I received strength from His presence, power from His Spirit; I received His life to make my own. Sealed with His touch with His hand upon my head, with fresh oil from heaven, He anointed me to flow.

> *Our fathers had the tabernacle of witness in the wilderness, as He appointed, instructing Moses to make it according to the pattern that he had seen, ⁴⁵which our fathers, having received it in turn, also brought with Joshua into the land possessed by the Gentiles, whom God drove out before the face of our fathers until the days of David, ⁴⁶who found favor before God and asked to find a dwelling for the God of Jacob. ⁴⁷But Solomon built Him a house. ⁴⁸However, the Most High does not dwell in temples made with hands.*
> **Acts 7:44-48**

Chapter 4

Life in His Presence

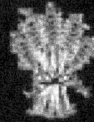

Speaking to one another in psalms and hymns and spiritual songs, singing and making melody in your heart to the Lord, [20]giving thanks always for all things to God the Father in the name of our Lord Jesus Christ, [21]submitting to one another in the fear of God. **Ephesians 5:19-21**

Making Melody

By Kofi

Life is a melody of song played on the strings of our testimonies. The harmony of goodness and mercy reveals a burning passion to celebrate the joy of the heart that can not be expressed in any other way but the singing of melodies. The sweet melodies are the testimonies of life played from the strings of the heart of man. The strings of faith, hope and charity combine to make one song, *"the testimony of praise"*. The melody of praise is an invitation for God to join us in our place of habitation; in the secret chambers of our being for a celebration of gratitude. When our hearts begin to create melody, heaven bows down to embrace the face of the earth and we are raptured in a moment's time.

The melodies of my heart exude a passion of love enraptured in the presence of God. I abide in Him and He abides in me and anoints me with fresh oil to testify of His power. The fragrance of His presence delivers the sweet aroma of His grace. While embracing in love overwhelmed with joy, my heart of tears fluttered to capture this moment in time. My mind is bypassed, my senses fail to respond and my lips tried to utter what fluttered from within. My tongue began to vibrate with lips stammering out of control. There are no discernable words to articulate, but they are words of rhythms that speak the melody of my heart. It is the melody of praise.

I hear a voice singing from within with rhythms of a trumpet singing in my ear. The trumpet begins to play a trilogy of song; it is the Father, Son and Holy Ghost combining in song streaming into my spirit a melody of praise. The spirit in me begins to shout with a power that shakes the rocks of my foundation. I began to tremble but I am not moved. I can feel the wind passing through me that ushers in overwhelming peace. The Voice of Peace speaks to my spirit; *"be still and know that I am God"*. My soul awakens at the sound of His Voice beckoning my spirit to embrace His song. Together we sing a melody of praise with my heart still overwhelmed with flutter and lips still stammering out of control. His song now becomes my song.

> *"This is my story, this is my song, praising my Savior all the day long."*

Our words became indivisible with my spirit and soul joined as one. I tried to speak what I could not say; with no words to explain the moment of my experience. My heart cried out, *"How can this be"*? Then my soul began to testify. I witnessed your heart fluttering; I witnessed the stammering of your lips; I witnessed the voice of the trumpet singing melodies in your ear. Suddenly, I heard the voice of the trumpet with my heart free from flutter and lips poised to speak. Then the fingers of my spirit began to play strings of melody from my heart. With joy unspeakable, my heart began to sing the melodies of praise; my spirit began to dance to the rhythms of my song. My soul testified, *"You are a witness"* and rested in peace!

Psalms, hymns, and spiritual songs are the testimony of the Saints confirming God's grace and His power of deliverance. When we perfect one another, it becomes a ministry; *"the ministry of submission"*. It is a level of communion between the Saints where all things are deemed common, even our testimonies.

In our communion with one another, we bear the testimony of Christ extrapolating the gift of God's love permeating from the depths of our secret encounters. The power of that kind of love unveils a grace to *"submit"* ourselves transparently to one another. Love unites and edifies providing healing from the fellowship of communion.

We all may not possess the same talents and gifts, but we share the same power in testifying. When we submit to one another, it is an indication of our humility. The level of our servanthood indicates the level of our fear of God. To fear God is simply to obey Him. Jesus taught us the principle of love and commanded that we should love one another. Love generates from deep within and is manifested in a multiplicity of expressions. We receive spiritual edification not by the prescriptions or formulas of man, but by what is driven from the heart. What exists within exude outward to connect with the receptors of faith. Faith born in secret and seasoned with the salt of our testimonies, testifies of the power of God's faithfulness.

When we speak by the anointing of the Holy Spirit, there will be variations how He delivers. Our power to testify is dependent solely on Him. The Spirit gives freedom to operate in our gifts connecting others to our faith. The liberty of faith springs forth with a passion driven by love.

The testimonies of faith are tools of empowerment for testimony in the lives of others. When we speak the psalms, hymns and spiritual songs they become a prophecy to the hearing ear. We wear upon our garments the legacy of praises *"giving thanks always for all things"*. It is the power and grace of God in the name of our Lord Jesus Christ that gives us wisdom and knowledge to bring edification to the Body of Christ.

In the fullness of our testimonies, it is revealed that our testimonies are confirmations of God's answer to our prayers. We testify in our ministry of submission to one another, the power of His faithfulness. Our songs of hope give rise to the Living Word that does not return unto Him void. It rebukes the power of our fears and will accomplish what it was commanded to do! This is my psalm, hymn, and my spiritual song. It is my testimony from the reservoirs of my faith:

> *And most of the brethren in the Lord, having become confident by my chains, are much more bold to speak the word without fear.* **Philippians 1:14**

The Holy Spirit will give us boldness to speak with a power to overcome all of our fears. Persecution can arise and our voices will be silenced in chains just as Paul and Silas were bounded by fetters of iron. God can orchestrate a deliverance by an exhibition of our faith in the believing power of prayer and praise within our captivity. The confidence by our chains will create a lasting testimony of a greater boldness to speak in our battles of faith.

Worship is a Life of Sacrifice

> *After Jesus was born in Bethlehem in Judea, during the time of King Herod, Magi from the east came to Jerusalem ²and asked, "Where is the one who has been born king of the Jews? We saw his star in the east and have come to worship him." ³When King Herod heard this he was disturbed and all Jerusalem with him.*
>
> *⁹After they had heard the king, they went on their way, and the star they had seen in the east went ahead of them until it stopped over the place where the child was. ¹⁰When they saw the star, they were overjoyed. ¹¹On coming to the house, they saw the child with his mother Mary, and they bowed down and worshipped Him. And when they had opened their treasures, they presented gifts to Him: gold, frankincense, and myrrh.* **Matt. 2:1-11**

Scripture says that the wise men sought Jesus when *"they saw His star in the East"*. What they saw was revealed by divine revelation but was hidden from Herod the King whose intentions were to destroy the promise of God. The enemy comes only to steal, kill, and destroy. Despite their titles, positions, and level of authority, the enemy's intention remains the same. Beware! For every revelation from God, there is always resistance that attempts to vacate His desire. The enemies of God will battle tooth and nail to contradict the plans that Jesus has for our lives. You have heard the scripture *"without a vision, the people perish"*. Vision is the Holy Grail of God's prophetic blueprint for our generation. It serves as the copy and shadow of heavenly things that are to be fulfilled in the earth.

Why did the wise men seek Jesus? They came to *worship* Him! They worshipped on bended knee, the ultimate act of submission. If men would bow their knee, they will discover a level of grace that can not be acquired any other way. Worship is fulfilled in our gifts, the sacrifice of those things that are so precious to us. The act of submission is accomplished in three parts; our submission in exchange for His authority, trust in the investment of our gifts and surrendering of our substance for His provisions.

Have you discerned the revelation of Jesus in your time? Has that *star* appeared to you? Has it brought you to that place of divine encounter with Him that we call "worship"? Worship is a prelude into the deeper dimensions of God and is fully accomplished in our sacrifice. Only in the presence of the Lord will we receive the revelation of His plans and purposes for our time. Through this divine encounter with Him, we will discover His character and be brought into the light of the revelation of His heart.

We find that the intentions of Herod were somewhat different than the wise men. His heart was bound with the cords of the wicked and the deception of worship was accomplished in his plans. In the seasons of God's revelation, contradictions and deceptions will emerge to resist His prophetic intentions. When faith emerges in pursuit of truth, there will always be an attempt to deny the fulfillment of His word. The pride of Herod was threatened at the emergence of faith that pursued the revelation of prophecy. God is the Father of faithfulness and truth demonstrated by the things that He reveals and performs in our times. The inclination of our heart is driven in humility to render an acceptance of His faithfulness by worship. Worship is an action of an undivided heart that connects our inward motivations to the source of our faith.

The threatening of Herod was no different than Lucifer who wanted his kingdom higher than the Kingdom of God.

> *And war broke out in heaven: Michael and his angels fought with the dragon; and the dragon and his angels fought, ⁸but they did not prevail, nor was a place found for them in heaven any longer.*
> **Revelations 12:7-8**

Lucifer fell, one-third of the angels fell, Adam fell, and now man has fallen. Heaven is a place of turbulence for God is always creating. In the center of His Kingdom where He sits with Jesus on His right hand and grace and mercy on the left is a place of absolute peace and serenity. It is a place where all things are perfect without spot or blemish. The order of heaven must be maintained and defended by the might of His power.

We Worship in Private-We Praise in Public

> *"O come, let us worship and bow down, let us kneel before the Lord our God our Maker."* **Psalm 95:6**

Worship is the ultimate destination of prayer. It takes us beyond the thoughts of all God's wonderful blessings and promises to commending Him for His person, character, attributes and perfection. We encounter Him in secret places, yielded, yearning to rendezvous with His presence. Humbled and submitted, we experience a peace that brings strength to our weary souls. You will not find the solace of His Spirit if you are standing in pride. As the wise men bowed down and knelt before Him, they submitted under His authority. As an empty vessel, when we encounter His presence in our submissions, we will discover His grace and mercy that He has purposed for our lives.

Worship is the *"way back"* into God's eternal presence. It is the sacrifice of our obedience. We are like the *"sankofa bird"*, moving forward in our efforts to reclaim what has been lost in our past. The tree of eternal existence in the presence of the Lord still remains, waiting, calling as a beckon on the hill to the ships of Zion that are lost in the turbulence of time. Inwardly, our hearts yearn for the fulfillment that only His presence can give.

My wife, Mary, has always had a passion for praise and worship. She became a teacher to me through the dark times of our struggles to fulfill God's plan for our lives. She applied the principles of faith, always praising with a song of faith upon her lips and worshipping with an undivided heart as a commitment of trust in all of our circumstances.

Mary's View

Worship is the key to entering the doorway of the Holy of Holies. It is the act of our heart, mind, body and spirit that will release the glory of God and the anointed power of the Holy Spirit into every area of our being. Worship is a sacrifice where we offer thanksgiving for His mercy, His grace, His goodness, His healing, His love, His friendship, and His favor and blessing. When the reality of His love, mercy and grace overwhelms us, His anointing will pour into us causing every fiber of our being to reverence and adore Him. As we renew our minds daily through prayer and the washing of the Word, we embrace the contract of our communion sharing His love with our hearts exuding in praise. It is then we will begin to operate on a higher level of victory and power. Our praise becomes a weapon of war that releases the storehouses of heaven on our behalf.

> *Enter into His gates with thanksgiving, And into His courts with praise, Be thankful to Him and bless His name.* **Psalm 100:4**

We enter into His gates with thanksgiving on bended knees. It is a time for gratefulness, an exhibition of our gratitude for His faithfulness. Our private worship prepares us for a public presentation of our secret sacrifices offered in a collective celebration of praise. In the constituency of the righteous, we celebrate our faith and offer the sacrifices of thanksgiving. It is not just a part of our church service that serves as a buffer zone for seating late arrivals or a wake-up call before the Word is brought forth. Praise is a testimony of thanksgiving, an expression of our heartfelt gratitude for all His victories past, present and hope in the battles before us. The *"sacrifice of praise"* is a concept that is foreign to the natural man who is void of spiritual revelation. Praise is an exhibition of our belief and trust in faith. The world's way of worry, complaining and fear of the circumstances of life are contradictions of our faith. The discipline of prayer, praise and worship creates a conduit to experience the fullness of joy as we rejoice through our circumstances glorifying Christ that His Glory will shine through us. Our testimonies are rendered as a power of our belief.

Praise unfolds into a greater experience of His power and we begin to worship when we touch the Heart of God. Scripture says in Psalm 22:3 that *"God inhabits the praises of His people"*. The presence of the Lord *"dwells"* in the atmosphere of His praise. It is not merely a reaction from an encounter with His presence; it is a vehicle of faith which brings us into the experience of His presence and power. Praise and worship are the *"gate-ways"* which allows us to enter the deeper dimensions of His glory.

It is easy to give thanks and praise when life is full of blessings. When we receive a promotion, finding the house of our dreams, money in the bank or when our barns are full; these are only temporary victories. Our communication line to the throne must always overflow with praise and thanksgiving from our weakness. Psalm 34:1 *"I will bless the Lord at all times; His praise shall continually be in my mouth."* Whatever circumstances life presents to us, we must maintain an attitude of praise. Praising God in the midst of our battles releases our faith with the assurance that He has the solution to whatever we are going through.

Praise Him in the midst of despair; when all is dark around us and we don't see an answer anywhere. Even, when life's circumstances challenges our faith, we must stand our ground and exercise the power of praise. This kind of praise allows us to rise above doubts and fears that robs us of the rewards of our obedience. Praise will cause you to rise higher in faith and get a fresh perspective of your circumstances through God's viewpoint.

Satan despises worship. He will battle our faith and can delay an answer to prayer if we allow it. The powers of darkness cannot tolerate the sounds of true praise flowing from the passion of our heart. It will torment their ears to silence. They will be repelled with no occupying place in the assembly of worship. An atmosphere which is filled with sincere praise and worship by a humbled spirit is an offense to Satan and his evil powers of influence. He fears the power in the name of Jesus and flees in defeat from the Lord's habitation of praise. Genuine praise and worship attracts the ear of God and will open the floodgates of His Heart as a river of love. He delights in His children seeking His Presence in an unconditional presentation of praise. He eagerly awaits the fragrance of our affections desiring to manifest His sweet presence and power in our midst.

The enemy to our faith has convincing power of the insolvability of our problems but the weapon he uses against us is null in effectiveness. When we activate God's power by faith in His Word and the testimony of praise in our mouth, the enemy will flee. When we walk in obedience to the instructions that Jesus gave us in His Word, we will see Him unravel our problems. God's people cannot be defeated if they will only learn to stand upon His Word in absolute confidence and trust; praising Him even when circumstances look the worst. The power of God is real and is always available, but we must demonstrate the ability to access His grace in the passion of prayer. If we pursue Him, we will be able to bring the demonstration of His power into our battles through the gates of His accepted praise.

Praise honors the sacrifice of Jesus in recognition of His obedience to fulfilling the word of destiny. It under girds faith as strength in our weakness and will bring deliverance into our lives. Praise is the articulated voice of faith and the proven language of angels surrounding the throne of heaven. With angels summoned at His power, He releases them to minister on our behalf.

The joy of the Lord is our strength and is proven in the power of praise. Praise brings strength to conquer and still the enemy of our destiny. For it to be activated we must understand the principle; "praise must precede, not follow blessings". We all have legal rights and access to the presence of God's secret power. When we have accepted the word of truth, the highway of faith will become a conduit to move the blessings of God into our lives.

"Let everything that hath breath, PRAISE THE LORD!"

Persuaded by Love

As I sit in this place of separation, confined to my Isle of Patmos, my heart cries out; *"Lord, make me whole again. Take not thy Spirit from me"*. It is the cry of a humbled spirit being separated from the power that only pure love can give. The heart is the center of our existence that channels life to every part of our body. It is the only organ that does not get a day off, neither should you desire it. It beats continuously delivering nutrients of love to every needed part. When the heart is weak, our very existence lay in the balance of its decisions. As the heart goes, so does our lives. Without the beating of the heart another deposit in the earth is made and the earth reclaims its balance by replenishing the soil from whence we were taken. The source of our weakness comes from the powers that have plagued humanity throughout the ages. It is the power of disobedience that entered into the heart of man which gave cause for sin to reign in our lives. The power was strong enough and overwhelmed man in the valley of his decisions disrupting the order of divine worship.

Worship is a principle commanded by the order of God's Word which requires our obedience; *"thou shall love the Lord thy God with all thy heart, soul and mind"*. If we remain in the power of God's eternal love, we can conquer every tempting power that tries to separate us from the love of our Father, even the power of our disobedience. The Apostle Paul wrote:

> *Yet in all these things we are more than conquerors through Him who loved us. 38For I am persuaded that neither death nor life, nor angels nor principalities nor powers, nor things present nor things to come, 39nor height nor depth, nor any other created thing, shall be able to separate us from the love of God which is in Christ Jesus our Lord.* **Romans 8:37-39**

Are you fully persuaded? Does the love of God dwell within the chambers of your heart so deeply that it is protected from all seen and unseen tempting powers? Or has the cancer of your disobedience, disappointments and self-condemnation entered into your blood stream and you have abandoned hope? Our hearts must remain guarded and resistive to any force that would lead us on a path distancing ourselves from the power that comes from the love of God through Christ Jesus. If we are fully persuaded, we will remain divinely connected by our prostrations of humility in continual worship of our Father. Disobedience has conquered the fallen and will continue to conquer you without the full persuasion the power of Christ brings into our lives. God developed a path back into His original intentions. Jesus said *"I am the way, the truth and the life, no man cometh to the Father except by Me"*.

The Blood of Jesus

When I received my conversion, I had a reoccurring vision. Every time I went into the prayer closet, I would experience the very same vision. It was a vision of me, bowed down on bended knee at the foot of the cross of Jesus. Tears were streaming down my face; my hands were cupped, yielding, thirsty, needing, wanting so desperately to drink of His blood. The blood came pouring from the wound of His suffering where they had pierced Him in His side. They had rejected Him, neglected Him and never respected Him. I could feel His pain and hurt in my own body. The cup of my hands began to fill with an unlimited flow of His blood and I began to drink. I was being cleansed with the power of His redemption and receiving His grace but more than anything, I was being filled with the power of His love. He loved me that much to feed His life into mine. I began to get so filled with His blood; His life was now becoming my life. The blood that flowed in Him began living in me. I partook of His presence and shared in His power to sustain suffering. When His Spirit left His body, it entered me. The life that was in Him is now living in me. He gave me a new name, "He called me His disciple". Now go! Do as I have done. They rejected Me, they will reject you. Take up this cross and never leave it! It will testify of Me of the love I have for you. After three days, He arose and released the power of His Help. I received the anointed energy He released for power to carry the cross.

I started my journey into the unknown not realizing the consequences of my decisions, but I was fully persuaded. After the visions discontinued, my mother gave me a word concerning my future, but I did not realize how experiential it would become:

> So Jesus answered and said, "Assuredly, I say to you, there is no one who has left house or brothers or sisters or father or mother or wife or children or lands, for My sake and the gospel's, 30who shall not receive a hundredfold now in this time houses and brothers and sisters and mothers and children and lands, with persecutions and in the age to come, eternal life. **Mark 10:29-30**

Persecution, persecution, persecution! Little did I know the power it possessed; I know now! I refuse to complain. It was and will remain purposed for my humility. But there is a grace that accompanies persecution which has a power of its own. I have learnt and will continue to learn the power of

God's sufficiency that sustains me through every battle, every assignment for the sake of righteousness. But you better be right! God forgives ignorance but there is a penalty for disobedience. I remain bound by the constraints of my captivity to a desire that He has placed in my heart. The motivation of my passion moves me into compliance of a predetermined path to fulfill His will and calling upon my life. It is a path of faith that demands my obedience.

My journey from the foot of the cross led me in search of the revelation of truth back to the beginning where the Angel of God is still standing. The protector is still standing at the gate guarding that which is sacred and eternal; *"it is the tree of life"*. With the blinding light of the flaming sword swirling about, I can not see inside to know what He knows neither can I find my way to that place of His desire. There is only one way back into the Garden of God; *"purity and singleness of heart through the gate called narrow"*.

It is my desire to see heavenly things for the revelation of God in our times. My daily prayer gives indication of my hearts desire. I pray the words that were prophesied into my life; *"Call unto me and I will answer you and show you great and mighty things that you know not"*. Heavenly things can not be seen unless God opens our spiritual eyes to instruct us in *"His Way"*. When our intentions and the motivations of our heart are acceptable unto Him, He will flood our spiritual corridors with revelation that comes from an unseen dimension of His grace. He will give us His gifts to discern and His power to perform the works of His destiny. *"Blessed are the pure in heart, for they shall see God."*

Chapter 5

Trouble in Zion

I also will no longer drive out before them any of the nations which Joshua left when he died, so that through them I may test Israel, whether they will keep the ways of the LORD, to walk in them as their fathers kept them, or not. **Judges 2:21-22**

On one of my mission trips to Africa, I was watching a BBC documentary concerning the state of the church in Europe which by all accounts, is in a freefall decline. It was surprising to realize that secularism has replaced the traditional role of the church. The spiritual conscience and foundational principles have eroded to the point of disrepair.

When the anointing of God is removed from our presence because of our denial and betrayal of truth, we will enter into His judgment. So many have ventured down that road confounding His grace and bore the consequence of rejection. The broadcast alluded what had happened in Europe is a precursor to the events that will come to America. Yes, we are next to follow! We can see the signs of it today emerging within our culture. Spiritual pollution has fumigated and dominated our airways. Apostasy, agnosticism, pessimism, unbelief and the emergence of science to dispel belief in Our Creator has emerged as an obstruction of truth. You can see the evidence of our declining stature by the erosion of our moral base. What exist in the spiritual has a paralleling effect of natural consequences.

> *There is a generation that curses its father, And does not bless its mother. ¹²There is a generation that is pure in its own eyes, Yet is not washed from its filthiness. ¹³There is a generation oh, how lofty are their eyes! And their eyelids are lifted up. ¹⁴There is a generation whose teeth are like swords, And whose fangs are like knives, To devour the poor from off the earth, And the needy from among men.* **Proverbs 30:11-14**

We have turned into a materialistic society with our beliefs anchored in the fruits of capitalism. The board rooms of our churches have adapted the principles of exploitation and greed just as the secular world, always bigger and larger at the expense of a suffering generation. The spirit of competition contends from one ministry to the next. Hatred, yes hatred, greed, division and corruption are the earmarks defeating God's government upon our lives. Everybody wants a piece of the rock. The sad part is that we say we do it in the name of the Lord. The spirit of greed runs rampart from secular dimensions to the spiritual. The Body of Christ is suffering from atrophy; spiritually lean. We have lost our fat. Scripture says that the fat belongs to God.

> *And the priest shall burn them on the altar as food, an offering made by fire for a sweet aroma; all the fat is the LORD's.* **Lev. 3:16**

Our lives are intended to be a sacrifice unto God, offered as a sweet aroma. Prostrated on the altar of fire with no more savor to our sacrifice, we will no longer remain useful for His purpose.

As a nation, we only cry out when we are fearful. Remember 9/11? Remember the summons to every available God to help us? Because of fear, we left our spiritual doors opened and now the enemy has come, taken root and now bearing fruit. *"We've lost the sovereignty of the righteousness of Jesus here in this land called America."* How miserable we have become in putting our trust and faith in iron chariots!

> *Woe to those who go down to Egypt for help, And rely on horses, Who trust in chariots because they are many, And in horsemen because they are very strong, But who do not look to the Holy One of Israel, Nor seek the LORD!* **Isaiah31:1**

As usual, after the threat is removed from us, we revert back to the same behavior that was purposed to be a teacher to us. Sounds familiar doesn't it? Maybe we should take a season and feast from the table of the Book of Judges. God's longsuffering is not a forever thing. The word is a lamp unto our feet and a light unto our path. The guidance of the Holy Spirit will lead us in a path away from the concourse of calamity and the whirlwinds of destruction that await us. If we are truly God's people who are called by His name, our instructions are bound in the humility of prayer to seek His face and turn away from the error of our ways. This is our only recoverable path.

So are the ways of every one that is greedy of gain; which taketh away the life of the owners thereof. ²⁰*Wisdom crieth without; she uttereth her voice in the streets:* ²¹*She crieth in the chief place of concourse, in the openings of the gates: in the city she uttereth her words, saying,* ²²*How long, ye simple ones, will ye love simplicity? And the scorners delight in their scorning, and fools hate knowledge?* ²³*Turn you at my reproof: behold, I will pour out my spirit unto you, I will make known my words unto you.* ²⁴*Because I have called, and ye refused; I have stretched out my hand, and no man regarded;* ²⁵*But ye have set at nought all my counsel, and would none of my reproof:*

²⁶*I also will laugh at your calamity; I will mock when your fear cometh;* ²⁷*When your fear cometh as desolation, and your destruction cometh as a whirlwind; when distress and anguish cometh upon you.* ²⁸*Then shall they call upon me, but I will not answer; they shall seek me early, but they shall not find me:*

²⁹*For that they hated knowledge, and did not choose the fear of the LORD:* ³⁰*They would none of my counsel: they despised all my reproof.* ³¹*Therefore shall they eat of the fruit of their own way, and be filled with their own devices.* ³²*For the turning away of the simple shall slay them, and the prosperity of fools shall destroy them.* ³³*But whosoever hearkeneth unto me shall dwell safely, and shall be quiet from fear of evil.* **Proverbs 1:19-33**

River of Destiny

Wisdom from the book of Proverbs is a river of life through the unknown path of our destiny. As we drift through the times and seasons of life; even through the storms that floods our path, we will be navigated to the place that God intends by the ordering of our steps. The all knowing power of the Spirit illuminates our walk of faith into the principles of God's righteousness that will lead us to the place of His desire. Scriptures says *"the heart of a king is in the hands of the Lord; like the rivers of water; He turns it wherever He wishes"*.

A river constantly produces change and our lives will undergo the same to apprehend the fullness of God's plans. The boundaries of the river define the channels of our lives that lead us to the place of our destiny. For its power to be effectuated, the river must be harnessed in one directional flow. The Body of Christ is the river that exists under the apostolic government of God; one body with many different tributaries of the anointing. But our power has become severed by the lack of unity in a divided flow of separation. Some remain frozen in the still waters of past revelations while yet others venture further into the unknown depths of faith. The Spirit of God is always evolving and turning His movement to bring fullness to the Body of Christ.

I am reminded of a cruise I took in the unpredictable waters of the Caribbean. After a season of sailing in the deep and being bombarded by the turbulence of wind, rain and the swelling seas, the captain had taken us safely across the ocean being navigated by the big eye in the sky. God will always be our defense in a time of trouble. He will navigate us through the storms of our life to help and guide us to our appointed destination. Scripture says *"God will not forsake us neither will He leave us"*.

When we entered the straits of Cozumel, the captain stopped his engines not too far from the distant shore. There appeared a pilot ship that brought on board another captain that would navigate the ship through the straits to its destination. As we neared the docking station, there appeared tug boats to bring the ship into its final resting place. The revealing eye of the spirit will be a pilot to guide you into the specifics of His direction. He will not falter and allow you to stumble.

> *Who led them through the deep, As a horse in the Wilderness, That they might not stumble?"* **Isaiah 63:13**

As a body, we have many different members with a variety of giftings. Even though you may be the captain of your ship, there are new terrains that are best navigated by someone who knows the territory better and has the power to perform what God has tasked you to do. It should not be considered relinquishing of your authority but the wisdom to utilize the gifts essential to your destiny. When God releases a word into our lives, it is important to remember that it is not given for you to do alone. Jesus needed the help of His Apostles; the Apostles needed the help of the Prophets and Deacons. We should learn from the lessons of Moses who was burdened trying to do everything by himself.

Chapter 6

Discerning the
Condition of the Body

And Jacob said to his household and to all who were with him, "Put away the foreign gods that are among you, purify yourselves, and change your garments. **Genesis 35:2**

efore the corrective response of judgment can be implemented, we must have accurate spiritual discernment and a solid foundation anchored in God's prophetic principles. We are to discern the Lord's Body just as Jude was discerning the condition of the Church in his Epistle. We are obligated to stand as watchmen protecting God's investments with the protective shield of spiritual discernment operating from our gifts.

The principle of unity and love is the sustaining wall of our defense. The consequence of improper fellowship within the body creates the lack of discernment of its condition. The result of not applying this spiritual principle causes weakness. When we suffer from weakness, it indicates that we lack the anointing and the gifts it provides to bring strength and power to our warfare. Weakness also indicates a deficiency that has occurred in our prayer life. It is the enemy's plan to keep you disconnected from the source of your power using the little foxes to keep you distracted.

We often get carried off majoring in our minors dealing with trivial things. If we are not diligent in prayer, weakness will develop leading to sickness; then we will experience an open attack of the enemy. Prolonged seasons of weakness will cause a sickness that will diminish our defensive system against an onslaught that comes against us. Satan does not contend with our strength, but will wait patiently for an opportunity to penetrate after the first line of defense has been compromised.

Prayer will keep us fortified and built up in the power and strength of God. If we are not committed to prayer, we will open ourselves up to a higher level of vulnerability; *"sleep"*. Sleep is a place of dread, where we are out of position to receive any spiritual revelation. There could be a war going on, but you will not hear the bombs exploding around you. An intruder could have compromised your defense, but you will not hear the alarms screaming in your slumber. This is very dangerous place for a Believer to arrive. It will take the powers of heaven to awaken you.

> *Awake, you who sleep, Arise from the dead,*
> *And Christ will give you light.* **Ephesians 5:14**

There is a summons for the Body of Christ to awaken! My father continually echoes the cry of the times we are in; he says; *"we are living in perilous times"*. It is the sign of a wayward generation caught up in a world of materialism who have neglected the teaching of the "elders". Materialism is a distraction that will keep you occupied with the things of this world. It has a power to lead you into bondage and leave you powerless against a materialistic addiction.

In My Father's House

When we were children growing up in my parent's home, we were brought up in the discipline of what it means to be a family. The sharing, caring, learning, even fussing and fighting; we experienced the wrath and peace of what love and guidance brings. We were taught the importance of value and morality with the wisdom of generations past. There were three principles enforced in our lives for the survival and prosperity of our generation and generations that would follow. Education! Christian education, family education and secular education. I call these the big three, in their respective order. My father taught us that education was an extension of the family. What we learned at home would be what would determine our success in the coming years. He guarded us against the perils of materialism and the power it possessed in an unguarded state, could control our lives.

Where's the Bling

Christmas was a time of celebration but where was the tree? Where were all the ornaments of glitter and the mistletoe for our embracing? Why was the chimney sealed with no entry way for Santa and his nine disciples of reindeer? Where was Rudolph with the false light on his nose leading the way to bring presents of delight filling our hearts with joy? The relics and images of the tradition of man and his schemes to capitalize on our ignorance were not welcomed. They were in the homes of everyone else but not ours. No lights, no tree, no Rudolph, no Santa; just one gift. It was a gift of love that was given from the heart of my parents.

My father was an enemy to Santa and his elves of deception. He knew they came to take and not give. Santa and his cohorts only wanted money to finance the subtleness of their plan of becoming the new king. They devised a plan to lure the little brainless lambs to the slaughter houses of Macys, Pennys, Sears, Walmart and the prince of them all, "Toysrus". It was a revolution taking place in our culture; "the supremacy of Christ versus the manipulating power of man". Who has won? When Christmas comes around and the celebration begins, will you bow in worship and share the joy of *the King of Kings*, or will you bring your gifts of money as a tribute to the new materialistic king?

Christmas morning for my family was a time of worship, thanksgiving and praise. We entered the House of God content with the inner joy that only love can bring. It was a celebration of the life of the new born King who was ruling in our hearts. There was no room for Santa; didn't need a ride in his sled to fly me through the sky. I believed in Jesus and it was His life I was taught to keep close to my heart. It was His path to follow; not to the north with Santa and his reindeer but into the heavens with Him sharing a ride into the presence of the King. Those were mystical times I will always remember.

Just as with Christmas, we were in Church to welcome in the New Year. New Years Eve became a labor of love; praying, watching and waiting to celebrate God's faithfulness that would take us into the undiscovered path ahead. The times of waiting on bended knee for the ticking of the clock to strike twelve still lurks in my memory. I remember the songs, the harmony of spiritual songs that came forth with the spontaneity of instruments of hands clapping and feet stomping to make rhythm and melody in the Spirit. I remember the praises and hymns of testimonies being sung by the Saints. I still hear my Mother's voice singing:

> *"At the cross, at the cross, where I first saw the light and the burdens of my heart rolled away. It was there by faith, I received my sight and now I am happy all the day."*

Then the bells began to ring and the music began to play and people all around embraced with a hug and a kiss of pure love; a gratefulness to be alive and a hope of the blessings a new year would bring. A new year was ushered in with a new season of hope for the testimony of God's keeping power. It was a time to believe; a time to dream; a time to discover what was hidden in the path ahead. In the coldness of the night, after leaving the warmth of the sanctuary, I could see the stars above glowing in brilliance against the background of the deep unknown. The glow became a lamp unto my feet and a light unto my path leading me forward into the direction of new discoveries. It is imperative that we retain the knowledge of our teachings and never forget the sacrifice of our elders that created a pathway for our future.

From the stepping stones of generations past, the foundation of our future was established on the principles of love committed to our success. The love of Christ produces a unity where all things are common, even our faith. Keep the imperishable bond of love and faith will never fail us.

That he would grant you, according to the riches of his glory, to be strengthened with might by his Spirit in the inner man; That Christ may dwell in your hearts by faith; that ye, being rooted and grounded in love, May be able to comprehend with all saints what is the breadth, and length, and depth, and height; And to know the love of Christ, which passeth knowledge, that ye might be filled with all the fullness of God.
Ephesians 3:16-19

The new law in Christ Jesus operates on the principles of love that fulfills all law. Through the power of the love of Christ, He has empowered us with the inheritance of His Spirit to be sustained in His grace. The work of our hands must be finished for the work of liberty in the spirit to have preeminence. How can this be achieved? The baptism of the Holy Ghost! Have you received since you believed? The Holy Spirit is a witness of God's Kingdom. In order to establish His truth in the earth, there must be a witness that represents all that the Kingdom is. He bears the evidence and reveals the established truth from times beginning.

But God has revealed them to us through His Spirit. For the Spirit searches all things, yes, the deep things of God. [11]For what man knows the things of a man except the spirit of the man which is in him? Even so no one knows the things of God except the Spirit of God. [12]Now we have received, not the spirit of the world, but the Spirit who is from God, that we might know the things that have been freely given to us by God.
1 Corinthians 2:10-12

Jude the Enforcer of Righteousness

Remember Jude? We have not put enough spiritual significance to his ministry. If you would study Jude, you would realize the power of his gifting. His writings are the standard we should apply to the spiritual relevance of our time if we are truly to *"discern the Lord's Body"*. Jude discerned that the body was out of order and certain men, not all men, but ungodly men had crept into the Church and turned the grace of God away from what it was intended to accomplish. God still has a remnant dedicated to His interest and yielded to His performances.

Jude, a bondservant of Jesus Christ, and brother of James, To those who are called, sanctified by God the Father, and preserved in Jesus Christ: 2Mercy, peace, and love be multiplied to you 3Beloved, while I was very diligent to write to you concerning our common salvation, I found it necessary to write to you exhorting you to contend earnestly for the faith which was once for all delivered to the saints. 4For certain men have crept in unnoticed, who long ago were marked out for this condemnation, ungodly men, who turn the grace of our God into lewdness and deny the only Lord God and our Lord Jesus Christ. 5But I want to remind you, though you once knew this, that the Lord, having saved the people out of the land of Egypt, afterward destroyed those who did not believe. **Jude 1-5**

Jude says this message is to you; the called ones who are sanctified in God's righteousness and preserved in the power of Christ through the Holy Spirit. Jude demonstrated the effectiveness of his gifting by operating in the power of love. He realized, to communicate the things of the Kingdom must be ministered in the conduit of God's grace; grace to speak and stand in the righteousness that His gifts provide.

I am grateful to Jude for his testimony that continues to give guidance in conducting spiritual warfare. He was a watchman, defender of the faith, defender of God's ordained order, and an instructor of warfare. He started out writing a letter to the Church concerning *"common things"*; salvation! Salvation is common to all believers in Christ. If you would read carefully, you will discover that Jude never got to finish his letter. In the process of encouraging the Saints, he found it necessary to change the intent of his writing from that of common things to what was being revealed by the Holy Spirit. He exhorted the Saints earnestly to contend for the faith; *"defend your territory"*. Intruders had emerged and set up camp in the House of Faith.

The gifting of Jude was an early warning system of what was happening in the Church and what will happen in future times if we do not take corrective action. One of the most significant challenges confronting our Church today is the conflicting voices that make declarations of peace when it is a time of war. It is very difficult to see outside of yourself with a mirror that only reflects the image of your own conscience. It takes the discerning eye of the Spirit to bring recognition to our deficit of sight. The Church is at war but the revelation of our time is buried in the shadows of our pursuits. It is very dangerous to make spiritual assumptions with the limitations of our natural talents that shed no light on our present condition.

The Body of Christ is a spiritual organism. It moves, breathe; it has a pulse. It has needs that must be met for its survival. Revelation of those needs can only be actualized in the spirit which is the conduit for all of God's provisions. It takes a hearing ear to hear what the Spirit says. To be spiritual simply means that you are operating in the super-natural gifting that God's grace provides. So many churches today do not discern the difference between intellectualism and religion versus spirituality and the anointing.

Moses received the law which did not have the power to sustain the God life without the requirement of sacrifices. Much of the church community as of today, still operate on the written principles of the word without the inspiration the Holy Spirit provides. Tradition is limited to the performance of what the flesh can accomplish; the works of your hands. What was rendered as pleasing unto God in times past of our sacrifices is not a substitute for the requirement of faith that the Holy Spirit brings into our lives. The Holy Spirit anoints our gifting and talents as a sacrifice for service in the Kingdom.

Divine Order

God is a God of order that He perfected at the beginning of time. Lucifer violated a very important principle; *"stay in your place, do not usurp the order of the Kingdom"*. It caused a mass exit from heaven of one-third of heaven's angelic force. There is a serious consequence of frustrating the grace of God by defying or circumventing His divine order.

> *But these, like natural brute beasts made to be caught and destroyed, speak evil of the things they do not understand, and will utterly perish in their own corruption.*
> **2 Peter 2:12**

What is divine order? The word "order" is symbolic with the word "purity". Purity represents things that are in place. The tactical approach the adversary engages the Body of Christ is to attack the order of things; from the head down. When purity is compromised at the top, the whole body becomes corrupt.

> *If a ruler pays attention to lies, All his servants become wicked.* **Proverbs 29:12**

The prophetic blueprint of the Church is an exact replication of the image that God intended. An image or pattern is not the end of all things. It only serves as an instrument, a place holder for something of greater value. The blueprint of the Church revealed in the revelation of *"The Tabernacle"* is a fore-runner of the Kingdom of God.

We have majored in our minors for so long that we have distanced ourselves away from God's original plan by our religions, methodologies and secular beliefs which has led to confusion. The Church was never meant to be the end of all that He intended; only to be used as a weapon to facilitate His greater glory of the establishment of His Kingdom. The perfection of our obedience is purposed to lead us into the ultimate spiritual encounter as a people without spot or blemish ready to be offered as the bride of Christ waiting to occupy His Kingdom. Raptured in a moment's time, we will be changed to be as He is and know Him in the power of His love. This spiritual transformation will result in a confirmation of His glory. I call it a forever place; a place of habitation beyond resurrection! The Kingdom of God is spiritual superceding the natural boundaries of religion and our human perceptions.

> *Who will transform our lowly body that it may be conformed to His glorious body, according to the working by which He is able even to subdue all things unto Himself.* **Philippians 3:21**

> *I beseech you therefore, brethren, by the mercies of God, that ye present your bodies a living sacrifice, holy, acceptable unto God, which is your reasonable service. And be not conformed to this world: but be ye transformed by the renewing of your mind, that ye may prove what is that good, and acceptable, and perfect, will of God.* **Romans 12:1-2**

God's Word will transform our thoughts into His thoughts. He will order our conscience to know what He knows and see as He sees. His Spirit will unite to our obedience as we strive together to perfect His Word. The light of the Spirit of God leads us down the path of righteousness where all things are pure and spiritually harmonious. To submit to that order produces an honor. Honor defines the value, reputation, or worth of a thing both in the eyes of those who claim it and those who acknowledge it. Honor produces equality to the one who gives the honor and the one who receives the honor. It is an honor to serve and an honor to receive the rewards of our obedience. However, servanthood produces the highest honor. To serve is to honor and to honor is to give. Servanthood does not produce competition neither does it lay claim to one's greatness. It does not seek equality of itself but speaks with the voice that says *"I am least amongst you"*. It produces a level of faith that can only be acquired through humility. Humility is at the root of compassion that appropriates the needs for our lives.

The Holy Spirit is the revealer of truth and the preserver of the perfect order that Jesus envisioned for His Church. What Jude encountered was prophetic resistance that had crept into the church unawares. It takes the spirit of discernment to recognize and identify the motives, operations and every counter intention that the adversary uses against the Body of Christ. Jude professed an urgency in the spirit derived from his gifting that he considered necessary to address. As Believers, the necessary things of God, which are spiritually discerning should be of paramount interest to us.

> *To another the working of miracles; to another prophecy; to another discerning of spirits; to another divers kinds of tongues; to another the interpretation of tongues: But all these worketh that one and the selfsame Spirit, dividing to every man severally as he will.* **1 Cor. 12:10-11**

Prophetic Resistance and Insurgency

Prophetic resistance occurs when the order of God is being challenged. The discerning gift of Jude revealed a very unique example of spiritual opposition at the apostolic level of authority. Jude contends that certain men crept into the Church unaware, but he makes the statement *"you can fool some of the people some of the time, but you can't fool me"*. How could Jude see something that no one else could? Simply, we all have different gifting but of the same spirit. There is only one true anointing of the Spirit of God. I have spoken under the prophetic mantle in many of man's churches and encountered the resistive spirit of the Pharisees. Fortunately, in most cases, I was never given an invitation to come back. I will never fret on such a small thing because I recognize that God makes room for His gifts. I go where I am sent!

> *For there are certain men crept in unawares, who were before of old ordained to this condemnation, ungodly men, turning the grace of our God into lasciviousness, and denying the only Lord God, and our Lord Jesus Christ.*
> **Jude 4**

Jude's gift of spiritual discernment revealed the true desires of the adversary; lasciviousness. The ultimate intent of the enemy was purposed to frustrate the grace of God and render a people captive and ineffective in performing the things of the Kingdom. The elect of God can easily be deceived by the forces of darkness if we are not spiritually discerning.

Then if any man shall say unto you, Lo, here is Christ, or there; believe it not. For there shall arise false Christs, and false prophets, and shall show great signs and wonders; insomuch that, if it were possible, they shall deceive the very elect.
Matthew 24:23-24

Mockers

Jude referred to those who perpetrated dishonor as "mockers"; men whose intentions were purposed solely on perverting God's grace. Jude said these men were sensual persons, who caused "divisions" and did not possess the Holy Spirit. To operate in the things of the Kingdom without an anointing will only produce perversions of God's truth and cause division as a result of violating His order. The discerning characteristics of a mocker are those who treat you with contempt purposed to bring disappointment to the hope of fulfilling your destiny. You can discern their imitations and disguised counterfeit appearance by the false anointing manufactured out of their fleshly desire.

But you, beloved, remember the words which were spoken before by the apostles of our Lord Jesus Christ: how they told you that there would be mockers in the last time who would walk according to their own ungodly lusts. **Jude 17-18**

Cain-Balaam-Korah

Woe unto them! for they have gone in the way of Cain, and ran greedily after the error of Balaam for profit, and perished in the rebellion of Korah. **Jude 11**

120

Jude decreed a judgment upon those who had turned the grace of God into greed. Woe unto them! Just as pride, greed will blind you and open the door for curses that will attach to your destiny. The way of Cain is symbolic of those who have gone in the way and know the way of righteousness but allow sin to rule over them. Those who ran greedily after the error of Balaam for profit are represented as false prophets who are accused of spiritual merchandising. Be careful who you follow for you could be following someone who is operating in *"the error of Balaam"* and you could suffer the same consequence. There is a deception in walking in the titles and accolades of man. Pride will diminish your spirit and your flesh will be consumed in greed. Greed for name and fame; greed for what the gospel profits you; greed for the children's bread. What would it profit you to gain the whole world and lose your soul?

The rebellion of Korah is synonymous with those who thrust themselves into the priesthood and rebel against the authority and order of God. I have seen the exploitation of intellectualism replacing the sovereignty of the Holy Spirit's dominion in the Church. The prophetic formulas rendered by man to achieve success only served as a tool of deception to conquer and exploit the resources intended for God's Kingdom. Our prosperity is secured in our obedience to God's instruction for our lives and not in the manipulation of a word in exchange for money. Beware of familiar spirits. If you are not discerning, *"they will know what you don't know"*. The works of our hands has finished and there is nothing to be acquired beyond the provisions of faith. The Church of the Lord Jesus Christ belongs to the people of

God existing under the authority of the Holy Spirit. It is the inheritance of a future kingdom.

Some years ago, I was preparing a church letter to be sent to all of our partners. In the salutation, I had written the words *"pastor and founder"*. The Mother of the Church came to me to render correction of my error. In the rebuke of her words, I was brought to understand that *"I was not the founder; Jesus found me"*! Enough said; I immediately made the correction. Some of us operate on the fringe of the law beyond what is expedient. The arrogance of our success should not give the appearance of an offense but should be shadowed in humility. Scripture says we are to *"abstain from the appearance of corruption, exploitation and evil"*.

At the very beginning, I spoke with my daughter and told her of my intent to start an outreach ministry. I expressed my desire to help the young people that were disenfranchised, struggling spiritually and economically. She had just one word for me; *"Dad make sure that you get your Mercedes before you start your work"*. Wisdom received! I am still clothed in camel's hair feasting on a buffet of locust and wild honey. She had seen the abuse and misappropriations of the provisions that God had released for His people redirected to serve the desires of man. She understood the principle of all things being common in the household of faith; common in our giving and in our receiving. I don't hear the testimony of Ananias and Sapphira being echoed from our pulpits as I have in the past. Is it because of the accumulated wealth of our super heroes? What is good for the goose is good for the gander. You do remember how Ananias sold a possession and kept back part of the price of the land for himself and lied to the Holy Ghost? The convenient schemes of man hide behind the powers of the constitution separating the church from state to mask his greed. The Holy Spirit will bring exposure to all his actions when it pertains to the Kingdom of Christ.

> *All things are lawful for me, but not all things are expedient; all things are lawful for me, but not all things edify.*
> **1 Corinthians 10:23**

Spiritual Warfare

> *But ye, beloved, building up yourselves on your most holy faith, praying in the Holy Ghost, Keep yourselves in the love of God, looking for the mercy of our Lord Jesus Christ unto eternal life. And of some have compassion, making a difference: And others save with fear, pulling them out of the fire; hating even the garment spotted by the flesh. Now unto him that is able to keep you from falling, and to present you faultless before the presence of his glory with exceeding joy.* **Jude 20-24**

Jude gives a road map into the spiritual dimensions of prayer. There is something that we need to do for ourselves that no one else can do for us and that is to *"build ourselves up in prophetic prayer".* The solution is simple; "Pray in the Holy Ghost". As long as we remain in the love of God, we will find the grace and mercy needed to keep us from falling. It is through the communion and the fellowship of the Spirit that we find grace. When we engage God praying in the

Holy Ghost, we enter into intercession with Him; a spiritual agreement where we come to know His heart and His intention for our lives.

My House Shall Be Called a House of Prayer

When Jesus was baptized, He prayed and the result of His prayer "opened heaven" and the revelation of God manifested. We are the living tabernacle of God in the Spirit; the true House of God. Jesus said *"My house shall be called the House of Prayer"*. The development of our prayer life leads to a deeper relationship and love for our Father.

> *Call unto me and I will answer you and show you great and mighty things that you know not.* **Jeremiah 33:3**

> *And it came to pass in those days, that he went out into a mountain to pray, and continued all night in prayer to God. And when it was day, he called unto him his disciples: and of them he chose twelve.* **Luke 6:12-13**

Jesus continued in prayer. We are instructed to pray without ceasing. When we pray in the Spirit, our prayer will transform prophetically into a prophecy. And when we speak those things that we hear from God, there will be healing, deliverance and restoration. We will experience resurrection power gained through fellowship with Him. The principle of seeking God through prayer says that if we seek Him we will find Him and we will discover His grace.

Chapter 7

**Revolution
Making of a Whip**

When He had made a whip of small cords, He drove them all out of the temple, with the sheep and the oxen, and poured out the changers' money and overturned the tables. And He said to those who sold doves, "Take these things away! Do not make My Father's house a house of merchandise!" My house shall be called a house of prayer for all nations. **John 2:15; Matt 21:13**

Blessed be the Lord my Rock, who trains my hands for war and my fingers for battle. **Psalms 144:1**

There can be an excuse for ignorance that comes from the lack of knowledge. We all suffer in some way a deficit of knowledge of the things we do not apply ourselves to know. But the inherent nature of right and wrong is an instinctive law legislated upon the tablets of our conscience. When we violate this principle, we will suffer the cost of correction. When I was a child, there was one word I dreaded; *"whip"!* The whip came because of disobedience and not because I wasn't given instructions to make the correct determination between what was right and wrong. The whip was an enforcer, a regulator and judge to keep me disciplined in the order of my teaching. Surprisingly, it had the effect of restoring me to my right conscience.

Jesus used a whip to bring order to His House after all words had failed. That sounds familiar! You can preach until the cows come home, but nobody is listening.

A servant will not be corrected by mere words;
For though he understands, he will not respond. **Proverbs 29:19**

When man makes a decision to pursue his ambitions and dreams of glamour and fame, he will not on his own make the necessary changes to correct his course. The path of repentance is buried deep beneath the shield of pride masking his desires. Pride has an overwhelming influence that has crippled the heart and integrity of so many of the chosen. I have witnessed their fall as they elevated themselves because of their talents and exploits.

In the season of our small beginnings, a foundation of humility draws the weak and feeble to the wells of hope at our doorsteps. We minister to their needs out of the abundance of love and compassion. To some, we have an *iconic* presence that can lead to illegal attachments. Some exploit this weakness for their own promotion. When our character is contested, the imperfections of a calloused heart and our ill-fated desires will manifest the lower order of our existence; *"greed"*. Some will eat of the forbidden and the world of materiality will come alive. The spirit of this world will then lead some down a path of exploitation consuming the *"shewbread"* and developing schemes to consume all in their path, evolving into money changers and merchandisers. Pursuing a path unchecked, thieves will emerge stealing from God that which belongs to Him and stealing the children's bread they so desperately need. It is time now that we get fixed. *The whip!*

Whip of cords are the spiritual weapons used to bring restoration to the House of God. When Jesus cleansed the temple, He carefully chose specific cords to make a whip that were tried and perfected into an object of His desire. The whip is the symbol of a *"declaration of war"*. It is evicting time; evicting the government of man who has established himself in the dominion of God's divine providence. The whip also represents reclaiming rights of the Believer to take back and restore what has been taken from them.

The Church of the Lord Jesus Christ is the invested interest of the sacrifices of the Saints and not meant to be a haven for man and his corruptive practices. The distribution of the collected wealth has been redirected to those who propagate themselves as the greatest amongst us and not to the meek and humbled called to a life of servanthood. Our leaders are living in excess accumulating wealth beyond the provisions of grace. The competitive power of greed has strangled the hearts of so many of the chosen. Their ambition has driven them to accept the philosophy *"He who has the tallest steeple wins"*. They implement schemes to exploit the weak and needy to build their projects rather than directing their resources to minister healing to the hurting and deprived. The Church has power to eliminate poverty in our communities; house by house, family by family, child by child. But some will say *"it does not serve our best interest"*.

While in Ghana, I committed my interest to provide one hundred scholarships for kids to go to college. You would have thought it was a grand idea. I exhausted my resources only to discover there were those within the Church community who did not share my passion. From the highest level, politicians, pastors and the business community who had power to do were threaten because of control and power. Controlling spirits aligned with the pride of man's desire proved to be a dominate impediment.

Have you ever thought about how a whip is made? A whip is made of strands of hide that are strategically woven together. Jointly knitted together, they create a sound when activated into motion. It is the sound of judgment! Judgment has come to the House of God because of the manipulation of truth and the apathy that has followed. We are in violation of God's order which has caused an interruption of fellowship and communion between Jesus and His Church. The result has led us down a path pursuing man as the sole representative of Jesus in our time. The voice of man has shadowed the voice of God's eminence. The mighty are falling away and a new era of leaders will emerge that must apprehend the lessons from prior generations.

The Church has been operating in a spiritual deficit for quite some time because man has accomplished the desires of his pride. Where there is pride, he is left to do things out of his own energies. The Spirit of God will not contend with the self-will of man. A heart lifted up in pride can not sustain the weight of its own deception and will ultimately fall in defeat. Jesus said *"if I be lifted up, I will draw all men unto me"*. The banner of Christ's deliverance has been obscured in the wake of man pursuing his own destiny.

Jointly Knitted Together

The strands of the whip are woven together as an instrument of correction. Under the guidance of the Holy Spirit, it is implemented as a weapon of war to execute God's judgments to bring correction and change. The strands are indicative of the ministry gifts He has perfected to establish His righteous order in the Church.

Man continues to struggle in his attempts to make God's Kingdom his kingdom. Power and authority that operates outside the umbrella of humility brings exposure to the flaws of our character and will leave us vulnerable to deception as we stand alone in our pride. God gave man authority to rule on earth and created a habitation for Himself called the Garden. Adam began to rule under His protection and guidance to maintain His Kingdom. Like Adam, we have made the fatal mistake of perverting that which was sacred and holy by falling prey to seducing spirits. The pride of disobedience still contends with our faith. Just as Adam failed in the rulership of the Garden; today the struggle of the rulership of the Holy Spirit contends with the hearts of man in the House of Faith. We can never be equal to the task of God's authority of the Holy Spirit who has been given all authority in the Church.

God intended His Church to operate under the power and guidance the Holy Spirit provides. Today we are no different than in the days of Simon recorded in the Book of Acts who said *"give me this power that whoever I lay hands on, will receive the Holy Ghost"*. The offer was an attempt to exchange God's spiritual gifting for money. We call that merchandising. The judgment rendered upon Simon will be no different than the judgment upon us. There is a perishing effect to believe that an anointing can be purchased with money or the acquisition of grace can be achieved by a material substitute. Some Believers attach themselves to the celebrity of man hoping to receive spiritual gifts and positions in exchange for their loyalty of contributions. The Apostle Peter referred to this as *"wickedness"*. Greed and the thirst for more than God's provision is an indication of a deficit in man's heart. It reveals a compromise that has corrupted his character and integrity. The boundaries of our aspirations should limit us to the boundaries of grace. A desire beyond grace is an illusion embedded in the path of deception that has no defining end.

> For the weapons of our warfare are not carnal but mighty in God for pulling down strongholds, 5casting down arguments and every high thing that exalts itself against the knowledge of God, bringing every thought into captivity to the obedience of Christ, 6and being ready to punish all disobedience when your obedience is fulfilled. **2 Corinthians 10:4-6**

At the sound of the crack, it is a clarion call for judgment. Jesus uniquely fabricated each individual strand, cut and altered to produce the sound of His judgment. It is God's prerogative to shape and fashion our lives according to His design to maximize on His investment in us. Our gifts are the measured good of His intentions. We all have been empowered with a measure of His gifting to accomplish whatever our instructions have determined necessary to perform. Despite the uniqueness of each strand, they come together with a readiness to revenge all disobedience only after our obedience is fulfilled. Not every strand is chosen; only those that are called in agreement to the task of reclaiming the spiritual conscience of the Spirit. The sound of the crack generates the voice of judgment, a prophetic call to bring restoration to the House of Faith.

As a light of His countenance, we are committed to maintaining prayer in the habitation of the righteous. Prayer is our GPS, *"God's Positioning System"*. God is our transmitter and we are the receivers. He positions our lives to the time and intersection of His destiny. He is our guiding light when we have no visibility and warns us in times of trouble. He will bring answers to our questions concerning our destiny. Just like the GPS, the requirement of faith says that we must always keep our switch activated accepting the instructions purposed to lead us in the right path. Our batteries must always be charged rejuvenating our prayer life to secure our connection from failure and our antennas constantly pointing upward, indicating our trust and hope into His guidance for our future.

Jesus had to cleanse the temple twice during His ministry; at the beginning and at the end. Sometimes, we as Believers have a hearing problem with an inability to retain past lessons. We tend to forget in the midst of our comfort and distractions the painful consequences that correction brings. What has been missing is a house devoted to prayer that will bring us into the true presence of God. It is the House Jesus envisioned as a power center of faith that captures the fragrance of our prayers.

> *I drew them with cords of a man, with bands of love: and I was to them as they that take off the yoke on their jaws, and I laid meat unto them.* **Hosea 11:4**

The cords of the whip are drawn out of God's love. We need to be reminded *"God will never leave us or forsake us, but He will correct us"*. He continues to involve Himself in our destiny.

> *My son, do not despise the chastening of the LORD, Nor detest His correction; [12]For whom the LORD loves He corrects, Just as a father the son in whom he delights.* **Proverbs 3:11-12**

The cords are braided together to centralize the power for our chastening and correction for maximum impact. When we as a body become unified, of one accord, one mind, one body, and one spirit; we will manifest the shared energy of a transforming anointing to accomplish mighty exploits. The vision of God is a Kingdom but man has reduced the expectation from a *"House of Prayer to a den of thieves"*.

It Takes Seasoning

In the hands of one who is seasoned in the power and wisdom of the Spirit, the whip can be a very powerful weapon. If you are not perfected in its use and guidance to the point of delivery, you will be humbled by tearing your own flesh. The correction of obedience will begin with you. We have been fabricated as weapons of God's righteousness to implement His plans. As stewards over His interest, we are to maintain His order and adjudicate the actions of His Spirit. When we have finally matured, we will release through the synergy of agreement a power of *"one putting a thousand to flight, but two putting ten thousand to flight"*.

Chapter 8

Revelation
Discernment

When Jesus came into the region of Caesarea Philippi, He asked His disciples, saying, "Who do men say that I, the Son of Man, am?" So they said, "Some say John the Baptist, some Elijah, and others Jeremiah or one of the prophets." He said to them, "But who do you say that I am?" Simon Peter answered and said, "You are the Christ, the Son of the living God." Jesus answered and said to him, "Blessed are you, Simon Bar-Jonah, for flesh and blood has not revealed this to you, but My Father who is in heaven. **Matthew 16:13**

Heaven is a spiritual place. The knowledge of God's plans and purposes can only be accessed by revelation knowledge revealed by His Spirit. To know heavenly things require spiritual ears empowered to discern, understand and reveal what the Spirit is saying as a result of our spiritual connection in prayer. *"God is a Spirit and they that worship Him must worship Him in spirit and in truth"*. In order to know the heart of God, we must be in constant communion with Him. The Kingdom of God is founded upon the principle of prayer and fellowship that produces revelation knowledge where He unveils His heart in our secret communion with Him. Fellowship is the root access to spiritual revelation where we encounter the passion of God at the center of His desire and receive the discernment of His will. Fellowship produces revelation; revelation produces a performance of our secret encounters. Apostle Peter received the blessing of Jesus as a result of his fellowship and received divine revelation.

"Jesus Christ the Chief Cornerstone"

And I also say to you that you are Peter, and on this rock I will build My church, and the gates of Hades shall not prevail against it. And I will give you the keys of the kingdom of heaven, and whatever you bind on earth will be bound in heaven, and whatever you loose on earth will be loosed in heaven. Then He commanded His disciples that they should tell no one that He was Jesus the Christ. **Matthew 16:20**

To unlock any door you must have access to the keys that controls the gateway. Jesus promised that the keys necessary to unlock the Kingdom of Heaven would be given with delegated authority to exercise power over all the abilities of the enemy. The exploits necessary to advance the Kingdom here on earth will only manifest through a proper spiritual relationship developed in a productive prayer life.

"The weapons of our warfare are not carnal but SPIRITUAL for pulling down of strongholds."

The weapons of our warfare are not of this world. If we are to effectively engage in spiritual warfare, we have to maintain constant communion to the source of our abilities. The keys of the Kingdom can and will only be effective when we demonstrate an ability to skillfully exercise authority in our prayer life. *"Whatever you bind here on earth is bound in heaven and whatever you loose on earth is loosed in heaven."* We have been given authority and the power over

138

demonic agents and every power of darkness that oppose our destiny to usher in the things necessary for our advancement. Spiritual authority without spiritual power is not sufficient to engage the craftiness of the adversary.

Method Man

Have you ever heard of *"method man"*? Neither have I; just a name I dreamed up. Method man is a philosopher of words who interprets spiritual revelations with the *"logic of his intellectualism"*. He is a strong man full of the wisdom of man's words. He will facetiously contend with you just to hone his skills. He does not realize that he is bound by his own deception; bound to failing practices that has no power to deliver him. He is gripped by a *"stronghold"*. Strongholds are any pre-existing practices, religions and methodologies that have opposed the advancing of the Kingdom.

Apostolic Foundation

> *And are built upon the foundation of the apostles and prophets Jesus Christ Himself being the chief corner stone; In whom all the building fitly framed together groweth unto an holy temple in the Lord: In whom ye also are builded together for a habitation of God through the Spirit.*
> **Ephesians 2:20-22**

The pathway of discovery leads us to understanding God's purpose. All biblical concepts reveal the blueprint of the Kingdom of God and His plans to bring an apostolic government to our generation. We have faltered implementing the discovery of this truth and are resistive to the necessary changes required of our instructions. The preeminence of our theology and practices which are not consistent with God's plan is a gross impediment to our advancement into deeper dimensions of prophetic truth.

The foundation of the Apostle establishes and adjudicate Kingdom principles to fitly join together all of the callings and gifts in the Body of Christ under the apostolic government of the Holy Spirit. It is a plan to bring order in His House that is purposed to perfect our development in righteousness. When the true Church begins to operate under the *"one-rule"* of the Spirit, we will have attained the divine expectations that Jesus envisioned.

The apostolic mantle covering the Church can not exist without the balance of the prophetic ministry. They work hand in hand. Every Apostle has a constituency of Prophets. The true apostolic ministries establish the order of Prophets who have the burden to carve out a deployment for the apostolic order. Prophets are sent as agents on assignment to proclaim a future action of the Spirit. Wherever God targets His word, he will send His Prophets in advance of any pending action. They are *"prophetic eyes"* unveiling spiritual revelations into the future. A diversity of gifting is poured into their ministry for the performance of signs and wonders by the Spirit of God.

> *And it shall come to pass afterward that I will pour out my spirit on all flesh; Your sons and daughters shall prophesy, your old men shall dream dreams, your young men shall see visions. And also on my menservants and on my maidservants I will pour out my spirit in thoses days.* **Joel 2:28-29**

The Spirit of the Lord reveals that He will do nothing in the earth, in our dimension of time and space without first and foremost revealing His intentions to those who He has chosen to be "His servant, The Prophet". He wants us prepared beyond any excuse to carry out His instructions.

> *Surely the Lord God does nothing, unless He reveals His secret to His servants the prophets. A lion has roared! Who will not fear? The Lord God has spoken! Who can but prophesy?* **Amos 3:7-8**

Secret Things

Scriptures reveals that *"these things were written for our learning"*. Despite the written testimonies, it requires a spiritual interpretation to manifest the true life of spiritual expressions. As we penetrate beyond the letter of the word, our learning begins at the point of encounter with God through divine revelation. Revelation is the revealed light of the Spirit bearing truth to the reality of hidden things, which man lacks the power to discover for himself. The natural man receives not neither does he understand the things of the Spirit. They are considered foolish to him. We are light bearers and the keeper of the burning flame of Christ that brings light to the world. In the book of Genesis, it is recorded that *"in the beginning God created the heavens and the earth"*. What does that mean? That He is the author of all seen and unseen realities. The heavens are invisible to us. It is a spiritual dimension that is the birthing place of all visible displays of God's creative power. He is a creator, the *"artist of our existence"*.

> *The secret things belong unto the LORD our God: but those things which are revealed belong unto us and to our children for ever, that we may do all the words of this law.*
> **Deut. 29:29**

Divine revelation is purposed to produce a testimony of His faithfulness. It is a promise to us that He is a faithful and a just God. He floods the power of His love into our lives to establish His rulership.

I was given a word some years ago by a renowned Prophet of God. He decreed God's blessings upon my life that I would inherit the same blessings that is upon his seed. He told me that *"I would never get too far out that God could not reach me"*. That is encouraging to know that my future is secured regardless of life's circumstances. I recall a time when my son and I were going to the county fair. Needless to say, my car broke down 20 miles from home. As we stood on the side of the road, flagging for help, no one would stop. I noticed a man and his son riding on bicycles coming toward us. He stopped and asked; "do you need any help"? I had one of those shoo fly don't bother me moments. My thought was how could you possibly help me on a bicycle? He said, I live right here. I will go get my car. *"Dumb is me"!*

He jumped started my car and said that he would follow me to make sure that I got home okay. Further down the road, the car stopped again. He gave me another jump and followed me to the repair shop. I thanked him and offered him some money. He refused to accept it. I asked could I give it to his son to show my gratitude and he agreed. After he left, I remembered the word of the prophet; *"I will never get too far out that God could not reach me"*. God had sent me an angel! I did not at first recognize the form that he appeared but had discernment enough to realize that He gave me the testimony of His word. His faithfulness remains true and His love never ending.

Revelation Knowledge

The Revelation of Jesus Christ, which God gave unto him, to show unto his servants things which must shortly come to pass; and he sent and signified it by his angel unto his servant John: Who bare record of the word of God, and of the testimony of Jesus Christ, and of all things that he saw. Blessed is he that breadth, and they that hear the words of this prophecy, and keep those things which are written therein: for the time is at hand.
Revelation 1:1-3

The prophet John declared that he was on that Isle of Pathos in captivity for the word of God and for the testimony of Jesus Christ. But there is something that we must pay very special attention to; he makes special mention that he also was there *"to bare record of all things that he saw"*. The purpose of revelation from God gives voice of His destiny as He releases His prophetic intent into our times. The consequence of our obedience will produce the blessings to those who *"read, hear, and keep the word of His prophetic instructions"*.

The power of the anointing brings knowledge through revelation and assigns the gifts of Jesus with the ability to interact with His Spirit. The power is just not limited to performing the miraculous, but through the grace of God creates an ability to live transformed lives as we are being perfected in righteousness. The Lord says *"ye shall receive power after the Holy Ghost has come upon you"*. That power translates into an anointing that will bring an apostolic revolution to the Body of Christ. The fullness of that power will only be realized when we are jointly knitted together flowing in the power of His love; the true *"agape"*. Then and only then, will we experience true resurrection power!

> *And to know the love of Christ, which passed knowledge, that ye might be filled with all the fullness of God. Now unto him that is able to do exceeding abundantly above all that we ask or think, according to the power that worked in us.*
> **Ephesians 3:19-21**

It is important that our ears are anointed to hear and receive the Lord's Word. What we hear, will have an influence on our spiritual perception. The more revelations we receive and demonstrate an ability to hear and do, the more will be revealed to us. Take special precaution who you allow to speak into your life. Those words are seeds and will bear fruit of its kind.

> *Take heed what you hear. With the same measure you use, it will be measured to you; and to you who hear, more will be given. 25For whoever has, to him more will be given; but whoever does not have, even what he has will be taken away from him.*
> **Mark 4:24-25**

Revelation simply means that God has removed the scales off our spiritual eyes. When that happens, we see things we have not seen before. The hidden things revealed by the Holy Spirit leads to the discovery of His will. The Word of the Lord *says "Eyes have not seen nor ears have heard the things that God has prepared for us"*. God desires that all of His children possess the ability to see beyond seen things. We walk by faith and not by sight. In the Book of Ephesians, the Holy Spirit indicates the necessity for receiving the spirit of wisdom and revelation knowledge.

> *That the God of our Lord Jesus Christ, the Father of glory, may give unto you the spirit of wisdom and revelation in the knowledge of him: The eyes of your understanding being enlightened; that ye may know what is the hope of his calling, and what the riches of the glory of his inheritance in the saints, And what is the exceeding great-ness of his power to us-ward who believe, according to the working of his mighty power.* **Ephesians 1:17-19**

Faith Love Prayer

> *Wherefore I also, after I heard of your* **faith** *in the Lord Jesus, and* **love** *unto all the saints, Cease not to give thanks for you, making mention of you in my* **prayers.** **Ephesians 1:15-16**

Scripture says faith, love and prayer precedes wisdom and revelation. Faith is the essence of the life of the Believer. There is power in faith supported by prayer that will supersede any of our past performances. Faith will move mountains and carve out valleys eradicating the power of unbelief. Faith is established upon the premise that there is nothing impossible if we exercise our will to believe. We have power to perform tremendous works in our day but we have fallen short because we choose not to believe. If you are encased in complacency, with all your needs met and no vision for the future, what driving aspiration could possibly lead you to the exercising of faith? I remember a song my Mother would sing; *"we come this far by faith, leaning on the Lord, trusting in His Holy Word, He never failed me yet"*. Those words are still true and will resonate throughout the ages. The new reality that God is preparing for us is being framed by the power of faith. The word He releases into our generation is purposed to frame our lives in preparation for the occupation of His vision.

Why Wait

One of my biggest battles has been learning the power of patience. It is a process that still continues. God's gifting upon my life is the prophecies of *"time and seasons"*. It is not every day He speaks His revelations of our future. If you would look at Elijah, when he spoke God's prophetic intent, he was quickly removed from the presence of all and ushered into a season of hiding, waiting for the next revelation. During this time, it can become a major test of your ability to master the season of what patience is to teach you. If you are not careful, you could develop bad habits, dealing with trivial things to occupy your time. The battle of the war of distractions can consume your energy. I have done some stupid things, all kinds of gimmicks to battle the oppressive forces that came to try my patience. When God confined Elijah to the brook, he was removed from anything and everything that could distract him. Patience is the prelude of humility. With patience, we acquire the obedience of waiting for the due season.

For a season, I have been living by the brook. With no more ravens to feed me, the brook has dried up and my ears are open to hear what the Spirit is revealing beyond my captivity. I have written my next book titled "Life by the Brook". It captures the life of patience and extrapolates the process of waiting. One of the prophets from Africa recently sent me a message. He said; *"it is time to shame the devil".* Its exhibition time! My time of waiting has ended with a word upon my lips to speak. The inscription upon my mantle says; *"in the time that is meant for you to hear, make sure you hear real good".*

Patience is something I should have perfected before launching into the deep perils of the unknown. However, sometimes in our walk, God creates a necessity of our faith and patience becomes secondary to His requirement. It can only then be developed in the process of our obedience in carrying out His instructions. The ministry of Jeremiah bears testimony of this; too early, too soon with little patience. Obedience is the only substitute for patience. If we perfect the instructions for our lives, patience will develop out of our obedience.

For years I lived the life of self dependency; very secure in my accomplishments and the comfort level it offered. I felt no need for patience because it was perfected in my ability to do what I wanted; get what I wanted when I wanted. I had natural talents that led me to the place of my *"seemingly"* success. However, in my progression, the acquisition of things became a liability to my destiny. I had to lighten my ship from the life of distractions if I were to accomplish the things before me. There is a spiritual requirement the Lord has given us all to do; *"master obedience to hear and perform His word"*. I often hear titles men bestow upon themselves as being "masters" of things their obedience has not achieved. Obedience will divide the waters of your life by testing the love of yourself versus the love of God that "He" shed abroad in your heart. Truly, if the love of Christ has liberated your heart, obedience will testify and bring to light the things that are most precious to you. I can always tell if the love of Jesus is perfected in someone by what they consider as truth. The words they speak; are they the words of men or are they the words of faith? Do they edify or bring condemnation? Are they about one's ambition or God's vision for their future? Whatever your choice may be, your obedience will follow!

Revelation is Conditional

> *What man is he that feared the LORD? Him shall he teach in the way that he shall choose. His soul shall dwell at ease; and his seed shall inherit the earth. The secret of the LORD is with them that fear him; and he will show them his covenant.*
> **Psalm 25:12-14**

Jesus desires to reveal his secrets to all of us. He gives them as an inheritance to our generations. However, His revealing is conditional; predicated upon our availability and our desire to carry out His instructions. It is recorded in the book of Isaiah *"if we are willing and obedient we shall eat the good of the land";* but if we refuse and rebel, we will be devoured by the consequence of our disobedience. God will make known His secrets to those that fear Him.

> *For God may speak in one way, or in another, Yet man does not perceive it. In a dream, in a vision of the night, When deep sleep falls upon men, While slumbering on their beds, Then He opens the ears of men, And seals their instruction. In order to turn man from his deed, And conceal pride from man.* **Job 33:14-17**

Revelation Produces Spiritual Discernment

Jesus desires that we receive not just wisdom to make one wise, but spiritual understanding that we obtain the knowledge of His will. The revelation of God produces a standard of spiritual character and integrity to increase our measure in the things of His Kingdom. Years ago, I had a consistent prayer for the spirit of wisdom. My Mother over heard my desire and interjected her wisdom. She said pray for wisdom specific for *"this day"* and not for the wisdom of time. The sufficiency of God's wisdom is a daily pursuit that can only be realized one day at a time. It is vanity to seek wisdom to make one wise without the counsel and favor of God's grace that is poured into our lives daily.

> *We do not cease to pray for you, and to desire that ye might be filled with the knowledge of his will in all wisdom and spiritual understanding.* **Col. 1:9**

Clouds of Revelation

> Jesus said... *"Whenever you see a cloud rising out of the west, immediately you say, 'A shower is coming; and so it is. And when you see the south wind blow, you say, 'There will be hot weather'; and there is. Hypocrites! You can discern the face of the sky and of the earth, but how is it you do not discern this time?* **Luke 12: 54-56**

Have you ever looked up and marveled at the clouds? Did you ask yourself "where do they come from?" Clouds are formed when water evaporates from the earth's surface. Before it can become a cloud, it must change its molecular structure from water to water vapor, light enough to rise and form a cloud. When a cloud is first forming, it is an invisible process to the naked eye. When it becomes visible, it is a finished process. We have given names to the different cloud formations and can determine the weather by the type of cloud form.

Every cloud has its own uniqueness. The only thing that is common to all clouds is "they are always moving". By the moving of the cloud, we can determine the direction the wind is blowing. *"But are you able to discern the direction of the wind if there is no cloud?"* You can see the clouds but can you see the wind that has no cloud? If your efforts fail you in this determination, I might suggest that you have no wind in your sail! An empty cloud with no rain is only a back drop to the infinity of space. The seed cloud of faith brings revelation through discernment of God's spiritual seasons.

In a moment of relaxation, I was sitting on the banks of the river watching the boats sailing by. I noticed as they entered into the inner harbor, they were being powered by the wind that filled their sail. The clouds were moving and gave witness to the wind. Faith is the wind of our destiny controlled by the rudder of the spirit to give us guidance. Spiritually, clouds are witnesses to the movement of God's wind. They give voice to the wind and hear testimony of His truth. Every cloud has a purpose. They are here for a moment then suddenly disappear. Just as the clouds, our spiritual life must undertake transformation. Our formations began in secret places; where the water was turning to vapor, hidden from the sight of man. We emerged from obscurity as the creative image of God with the habitation of rule by His Spirit. The Holy Spirit is the wind in our lives that directs us into the path of fulfillment. Just as the vapor of clouds collect in unity, we are the united good of God that He collects unto himself.

Scripture reveals that the early church was advanced because of persecution. When we are persecuted for the sake of righteousness, God's hand is never too short that He can not deliver us. What the enemy has determined for our demise will always work for our good. *"When the enemy comes in like a flood, the Spirit of the Lord will lift up a standard against him."* The clouds of God's anointing emerge with power and authority to combat the resistive powers of persecution that has hindered our advancement. There is a level of warfare that we must engage to contend for the faith. Spiritual discernment will unveil all of our enemies who are committed to wear out our faith.

> *For we do not wrestle against flesh and blood, but against principalities, against powers, against the rulers of the darkness of this age, against spiritual hosts of wickedness in the heavenly places.*
> **Ephesians 6:12**

A Changing Spiritual Paradigm

> *From the chamber of the south comes the whirlwind, And cold from the scattering winds of the north. By the breath of God ice is given, And the broad waters are frozen. Also with moisture He saturates the thick clouds; He scatters His bright clouds. And they swirl about, being turned by His guidance, That they may do whatever He commands them On the face of the whole earth. He causes it to come, Whether for correction, Or for His land, Or for mercy.*
> **Job 37:9-13**

We are in the midst of a changing spiritual paradigm. The swirling of the clouds has brought definition revealing God's intentions for our destiny. *"Whether for correction, Or for His land, Or for mercy";* we can only judge in part. It is being orchestrated from above turn by turn by His guidance. From the beginning, God spoke into the void of darkness and revelation emerged. It took seven days for this revelation to unfold; each day bringing forth a new dimension and demonstration of His glory. The clouds of God have again gathered together as a prophetic voice speaking into our time to reveal His intention. Hc has given us the pattern for the expansion of His Kingdom and the provisions of grace to bring true order to His House. It is very important that we incline our ears to hear the revelation of our time. The prophetic voice of the Spirit elevates above our pre-determinations we have accepted as truth.

The Body of Christ is emerging into a prophetic people. The book of Joel testifies that *"our sons and daughters will prophesy, old men will dream dreams and young men shall see visions"*. However, the path of man has led us by the wayside of the Lord's intentions. To correct the course of our past errors, it will require the diligence of prayer and our obedience. We have an awesome responsibility of establishing His blueprint. If we are faithful to *"hear and perform the words of His instructions";* the true sons of God will emerge with power and authority to reclaim the world. But our hearts must be pure pursuing His desire rather than the motivations stemming from our imperfections.

> *As for you, son of man, the children of your people are talking about you beside the walls and in the doors of the houses; and they speak to one another, everyone saying to his brother, 'Please come and hear what the word is that comes from the LORD.'* *31So they come to you as people do, they sit before you as My people, and they hear your words, but they do not do them; for with their mouth they show much love, but their hearts pursue their own gain.* *32Indeed you are to them as a very lovely song of one who has a pleasant voice and can play well on an instrument; for they hear your words, but they do not do them.* *33And when this comes to pass, surely it will come, then they will know that a prophet has been among them.*
> **Ezekiel 33:30-33**

Spiritual Understanding

It is important that we hear with clarity and can apply accurate spiritual interpretation of God's prophetic desire. We must constantly maintain a readiness to receive spiritual revelation of His intent. The knowledge of God's Word and the wisdom to accurately apply it will not be of any significance without spiritual understanding.

There are times our spiritual encounters with the Holy Spirit will lead us away from the beaten path where others have trafficked. The beaten path is a recycled path of familiarity littered with souls begging into the night searching for the shadow from the garment of the righteous to bring relief to their weary souls. They are often passed by without even a glimpse of hope. The poor and hurting will always be amongst us attaching their weakness to our strength.

> Now an angel of the Lord spoke to Philip, saying, "Arise and go toward the south along the road which goes down from Jerusalem to Gaza." This is desert. *27*So he arose and went. And behold, a man of Ethiopia, a eunuch of great authority under Candace the queen of the Ethiopians, who had charge of all her treasury, and had come to Jerusalem to worship, *28*was returning. And sitting in his chariot, he was reading Isaiah the prophet. *29*Then the Spirit said to Philip, "Go near and overtake this chariot." *30*So Philip ran to him, and heard him reading the prophet Isaiah, and said, "Do you understand what you are reading?" *31*And he said "How can I, unless someone guides me?"And he asked Philip to come up and sit with him. **Acts 8:26-35**

Philip met the Ethiopian eunuch along the way of the desert; off the beaten path and ran toward him with an eagerness to embrace an encounter of faith. Faith always reserves confidence for a supernatural performance of God's ability. When God gets ready to do something new, He will go where no man has treaded before. The greatest works of God are done in secret away from the distracting powers of unbelief and fear. When Jesus raised the damsel from the dead, He had to separate Himself from the powers of disagreement and familiarity. He cleansed the leper away from the beaten path because of the rigidity rooted in the bondage of religion. In secret, He healed the infirmity of the woman who touched the hem of His garment and was made whole by the power of her faith.

Philip discovered that the eunuch only had the logos, the written expression of God's prophetic intention in times past. But there was one thing lacking, spiritual under-standing. Understanding came by way of the revelation of Jesus which was prophesied by the Prophets of old. The experiential faith of Philip gave testimony of the power of Christ and His resurrection. Philip asked the eunuch *"do you understand what you are reading"*? The Ethiopian treasurer replied *"how can I unless someone guides me"*? To understand the prophetic Word of God requires an anointing as a guide into the deeper dimension of His revelations. Inquisition of the Spirit will always lead you into a greater expansion of the spiritual dimensions of the Kingdom. The consequence of the eunuch's search for truth revealed an understanding of God's prophetic intent.

Chapter 9

Apostolic Resistance

You stiff-necked and uncircumcised in heart and ears! You always resist the Holy Spirit; as your fathers did, so do you.
Acts 7:51

For every move of God, there is always resistance and persuasions that are allied as counter influences to bring contradiction to the *"Word of the Lord"*. They are parallel forces diametrically opposed to His mandate. Since the beginning of time, when God purposed to do a new thing in the earth, the imitative powers of Satan allied with the disobedience of man attempted to defeat His plans. There will always be winds of contradiction but they have no prevailing power over the Saints to nullify God's expectation. Power exists in the things that He says. He has the ability to perform every word of His intentions.

I love the writings of Apostle Paul. There is a level of transparency and humility that is quite uncommon today in our Christian community. It would benefit our church leadership to acknowledge their humanism with the humility that their trials and tribulations bring into their lives. Our trials are only purposed to produce a testimony of our walk of faith for the empowerment of others.

Years ago, I delivered a message to my Mother's Church. She told me that it was good and well received. She then proceeded to give me the wisdom of her day. She said to me "I noticed that during your delivery, you kept repeating the word 'you'. Change how you use the word 'you'. Preaching is to yourself first! We all eat from the same table. Let your words be about 'us'." We as ministers can never be above what we preach. Our lives are rendered as servants in the household of faith and His message is to us all. Eat your portion before you feed someone else!

> *For indeed, when we came to Macedonia, our bodies had no rest, but we were troubled on every side. Outside were conflicts, inside were fears.*
> **2 Corinthians 7:5**

Our faith will always be tested. It must be, has to be and will be! The power of faith always results in a testimony of the sufficiency of grace in all of our encounters. The synergy of faith and the creative word of the Holy Spirit bring confirmation of our warfare proving the word of the Lord is yea and amen. Trouble, yes trouble will come against us from every side. From the four dimensions of the spiritual hemisphere, we will be bombarded with conflicts.

Paul says our battles can be troublesome. The coexistence of our inner and outer conflicts creates challenges to our faith. Our outer warfares are the spiritual forces that are assigned to us as agents of defeat. Through Paul's transparency, we discover another war stirring within. It is the inner war of faith, the battle against unbelief. The lack of faith will produce fear. If we maintain a balanced prayer life to combat the forces that oppose us from the outside, we will not waiver while battling the wars within. Faith has an influencing affect on our obedience. If we keep faith attached to the word, nothing will become impossible to achieve. A focused prayer life and the persistency of faith, the Holy Spirit will bring comfort in the midst of our battles.

It is difficult to develop a testimony of faith if we rely on past experiences. It can create an opposing affect to your walk of faith. Peter on the Mount of Transfiguration wanted to build three tabernacles; sounds familiar doesn't it? Peter was reprimanded not to build on any other revelation but *"Jesus only"*. To build on past moves of God is a refusal to accept present day truths. The living dynamo of God's Spirit constantly changes, unveiling and establishing His truth.

Religion has its purpose; I should say pure religion. It gives shape and form of a static image. It's like a still photograph taken in times past that does not have the adapting capacity to display the moving cinema of life. It establishes a morality based on the principle of faith of what is considered the right thing to do. However, it is absent of power to provide the necessary ingredients for a life of faith to be maintained. It is like having a car without an engine; no power to move it. The law of religion was a pointer into the future of a living tabernacle for the habitation of God in the Spirit.

In the Book of Acts, the Apostle Paul wrote concerning the ministry of Apollos. It is a reminder to us that the Church must pursue the progressive revelation of the Spirit and our knowledge of truth should be based on accurate application of the principles. To accept any other truth is to accept truth in part. The result will lead to error and the path of error leads further into the bondage of man.

> *Now a certain Jew named Apollos, born at Alexandria, an eloquent man and mighty in the Scriptures, came to Ephesus.* *25This man had been instructed in the way of the Lord; and being fervent in spirit, he spoke and taught accurately the things of the Lord, though he knew only the baptism of John.* *26So he began to speak boldly in the synagogue. When Aquila and Priscilla heard him, they took him aside and explained to him the way of God more accurately.* **Acts 18:24-26**

Scripture says that Apollos taught to the extent of his knowledge but his knowledge was limited to *"baptism"*. He spoke fervently in spirit with boldness of his proclamations. To be fervent in spirit does not qualify you of having received the Holy Spirit. The Holy Spirit is more than goose bumps derived from a stimulated passion of the mind. Apollos taught *"accurately"* but there was a more excellent way. Aquila and Priscilla heard him speak and realized that he was ministering in the power of his flesh; no anointing!

They took him aside and explained the way of God "more accurately". This is a lesson we should learn, on the discretionary use of our gifting. Notice that the Word says *"they took him aside"*. Sometimes it is not what we say but the wisdom used in how we say what needs to be said. I will admit that sometimes because of my zeal and passion defending things concerning the Kingdom, I struggle to be as gracious realizing the dramatic affect the consequence of error could have on the lives of the fledging lambs who are not so advanced in faith and the defenseless sheep heading for slaughter like deer in the night stricken by light.

Many of our pulpits today at the Sunday hour are not operating in the full capacity of God's anointing and as a result the congregation suffers. Much of the power of God is lacking because there is a denial of truth for the sake of tradition which is indicative of those who refute change. The lack of knowledge is an instrument the enemy uses against us to keep us in bondage, enslaved to the letter of the law. The traditional spirit, as with Apollos, is absent of God's anointing and can only produce fervently with no power to perform. It is the Holy Spirit that has an accurate accountability of the testimony of Christ. There are times church leadership gets in the way of allowing the Holy Spirit to rule the Church. If this shoe fits, you might consider stepping aside before you are outside of God's grace.

> And it happened, while Apollos was at Corinth, that Paul, having passed through the upper regions, came to Ephesus. And finding some disciples ²he said to them, "Did you receive the Holy Spirit when you believed?" So they said to him, "We have not so much as heard whether there is a Holy Spirit." ³And he said to them, "Into what then were you baptized?" So they said, Into John's baptism. **Acts 19:1-3**

When John the Baptist came along, he began preparing the way for a more excellent way. He operated in a measure but the full measure of God's intent was realized only in

Jesus. John came along preaching baptism and indicated to us that we should not follow him, but the one who had the greater baptism; *"baptism in the Holy Spirit"*. Have you received since you believed? Or are you like the disciples of Apollo's *"we have not so much as heard whether there is a Holy Spirit"*. It is never too late. Ask God to fill your heart with the habitation of His presence

Move with the Spirit

When the door was sealed by the Angel of God, Adam had only one direction to move, "forward". We have a choice of moving with the wind of God or we can choose to remain in a place without His power. He will never lead us into the place of defeat! We must always respect the guidance of the Spirit as we charter in unknown waters. He did not bring us into a wilderness situation to die but to move us beyond our place of comfort. Before moving into the promise of something greater than our past experiences, we will be challenged in the area of our choices. Moses realized the consequences of moving on his own without the guidance and provision of the Spirit of God. Moses pleaded with God:

> *If Your Presence does not go with us, do not bring us up from here...*[18]*And he said, "Please, show me Your glory.*
> **Exodus 33:15,18**

Lord, show me Your glory! If we all would have the humility of spirit to recognize our dependency on the resources God's grace provides, our lives would be the richer. Our ministries would flourish reflecting light that has power to consume the hearts of men.

The evolving dynamics of spiritual change can create a measure of *"distrust and unbelief"*. But we must take the lessons learned from the discipline of Abraham; moving in faith and obedience to fulfill the words of our instructions. Scripture says that *"wisdom is found on the lips of him who has understanding"* but to attain to that level of wisdom requires an ear of accuracy. Just as God asked Ezekiel *"can these bones live"?* It was such a difficult thing for Ezekiel to envision having not seen the performance of God at that level before. We can not base our faith in what we see; only in what He says! Faith comes by hearing and hearing by the Word of God. Ezekiel's response was one of simplicity; *"only YOU know"*.

There are things that God envisions that we have no way of knowing and will not know if we do not hear and accurately apply His instructions. God told Ezekiel to prophesy, prophesy, prophesy. Speak what you hear ME say! When we speak what we have heard God say, it always results in a testimony of His Word. It produces healing, restoration and execution of His judgments wherever His word is sent to perform. It takes a hearing ear to manifest spiritual substance and translate it into evidence that says, "Truly, God is with me". When we speak exactly what we have heard HIM say, there will always be a performance of profound accuracy.

This is an area that is very troubling for many ministers of the gospel. They claim to know what they don't know. They speak what they have not heard. The level of God's revelation supersedes any and all knowledge past, present and future. The book of Ephesians records that the *"love of Christ passes knowledge"*. God's love is in another dimension of time and eternity. A life consumed in His love produces an intimacy where we come to know what He knows. Love sheds light on all secrets.

> *This Book of the Law shall not depart from your mouth, but you shall meditate in it day and night, that you may observe to do according to all that is written in it. For then you will make your way prosperous, and then you will have good success.*
> **Joshua 1:8**

What book has God put in your mouth? What were His instructions? Did He command you to speak or did He command you to hold your peace and meditate on what He has given you? Remember Joseph? We learned the consequence of speaking out of season. In some of our pulpits, we bear witness of the proliferation of words being spoken without the seasoning of preparation. To understand supernatural things, we need a supernatural connection. Despite the anointing upon our lives, unless God gives His energy to perform the power of our words, we become as sounding brass or a clanging cymbal. After the prophetic word is released, our requirement of obedience should comply according to all that have been revealed. Our obedience will bring an accomplishment that faith rewards as faithfulness. The word is a seed that bears fruit of its kind.

Discriminate Your Hearing

The heart of a man holds the treasure of his inner life. What saturates within our inner core is the substance of our character and spiritual fabric. My Father always said to me; *"I come to know a man by his words"*. What exudes from within is indicative of our moral and spiritual integrity. Words possess power. Some are spoken to edify and activate our faith while others when spoken are allied with the enemy purposed to bring condemnation upon us. Be careful what you receive that proceeds out of the mouth of men. What you allow to enter will have an affect on your spiritual stability. We must keep our ears inclined to hear what the Spirit is saying. He is our guide and discerner of truth and will bring confirmation to the things that we hear.

The Miriam Syndrome

> *Then sang Moses and the children of Israel this song unto the LORD, and spake, saying, I will sing unto the LORD, for he hath triumphed gloriously: the horse and his rider hath he thrown into the sea. The LORD is my strength and song, and he is become my salvation: he is my God, and I will prepare him a habitation; my father's God, and I will exalt him.* **Exodus 15:1-2**

> *And Miriam the prophetess, the sister of Aaron, took a timbrel in her hand; and all the women went out after her with timbrels and with dances. And Miriam answered them, Sing ye to the LORD, for he hath triumphed gloriously; the horse and his rider hath he thrown into the sea.* **Exodus 15:20-21**

The Miriam Syndrome? Moses and the children of Israel sang the praises of God for His power and glory that had been displayed by an awesome testimony of deliverance. When the testimonies of God emerge, there is always a counter influence. In every new move, there is always a challenge, either of demonic influence or human persuasion that usually manifest through familiarity. Familiarity is the root of contempt masked in deception as a false witness to the testimonies of the sovereignty of God's performances.

Miriam, the prophetess, the sister of Aaron, was provoked by the awesome work of God and the vessel that He chose to use to bring about such a mighty deliverance. She then rose up against the authority of God and entered into a provocation. As Moses and the children of Israel were praising in celebration of God's victorious power, she led an insurgency with all of the women. Notice that the scripture says that *"she answered them"*. Time out! What was the question? There was none! Miriam answered them but never joined in with them. Her response indicated an inner battle of the unrighteous judge that had strangled her heart; *"iniquity"*.

The seeds of corruption had been planted and brought forth the fruits of an unrighteous heart where jealousy and envy ruled. Where there is jealousy, you will find competition. The entangled energy of unrighteousness consumes and transforms our obedience into a heart scaled in darkness. The spirit of competition cast a shadow over Miriam's judgment; she was blinded not realizing that she was competing for the praises of God. Moses experienced the success of God's deliverance, but His success rendered a provocation for Miriam exposing the truth within her. That spirit prevails within the hearts and minds of so many Believers because of a failed battle of the Spirit to conqueror their hearts. There are those who echo resistance to the voice of our success when in truth, they are rejecting the voice of God that reigns supreme declaring His power over all the abilities of the enemy. For Moses, this was to progress to be a greater confrontation.

> And Miriam and Aaron spake against Moses because of the Ethiopian woman whom he had married: And they said, Hath the LORD indeed spoken only by Moses? Hath he not spoken also by us? And the LORD heard it. **Numbers 12:1-2**

We clearly see that Miriam truly has an issue; she also has company! At the root of her problem was the issue of authority; resisting the mantle of God's choice and how He chose to use him. Secondarily, the spirit of jealousy and competition arose suffocating the clear conscience of righteousness from her spirit. This explains why her judgment of leprosy was much greater than the judgment of Aaron. Every voice is not authorized to speak. It must be prophetically authenticated to communicate the things of God as it relates to His people and their destiny.

Light of Purity

Purity can not be contaminated despite how much we stain it. It is a revealer that amplifies the imperfections of a heart stained and riddled in unrighteousness exposed by the light of truth shining from within. Through the reflection of the word, purity is the mirror into the recesses of our inner chambers revealing the condition of our inner being. The next time you look at yourself in the mirror say these words; *"be true to thine self"*.

Lucifer, the son of the morning, son of the Bright and Morning Star, made a valiant attempt to overthrow heaven because of the imperfections that were in his heart. Scripture says;

> *How you are fallen from heaven, O Lucifer, son of the morning! How you are cut down to the ground, You who weakened the nations! 13For you have said in your heart: 'I will ascend into heaven, I will exalt my throne above the stars of God; I will also sit on the mount of the congregation On the farthest sides of the north; 14I will ascend above the heights of the clouds, I will be like the Most High.* **Isaiah 14:12-14**

We must realize, God is the possessor of all knowledge revealed and all things that remain hidden. He discerns the heart and calculates the motivation of our intent. There is nothing that escapes Him. David realized through experience that there are many plans in a man's heart but God separates His desire from ours and will only lend His anointing to those things that He has purposed. When we have lost our humility, we leave ourselves open for the strength of the flesh to gain authority in our lives. Our motivation then becomes more about 'I' than 'Him'. There are some in our midst just as Lucifer who have determined in their heart, *"I will ascend and exalt at any cost"!* Lucifer's desire was to establish his throne above that of God. He

170

didn't just want to be God; he wanted to be above God's omnipotence and the cloud of witnesses surrounding His throne. I ask myself, how is that possible? How could you ever become a covering higher than the glory of angels surrounding His Throne? It is vanity to believe that you can become greater than God's envisioning for your destiny.

Remember the tower of Babel where men united themselves to subvert the heavens? We shall forever exist beneath and never above. Eternity has no beginning and its end will never be realized. The time of your destiny does not include searching the ends of heaven. If you could travel that far, you will only arrive at the place you began. We are bound within the perimeter of God's creation abiding under the shadow of the Almighty, under His divine providence. The breadth and length of His covering is beyond the measure of our existence.

As Believers, we must maintain a level of contentment with our hearts aligned to God's purpose. As we look around our territory, we see men performing works of ministry and the desire to become something other than God's intent. If our hearts are not anchored and separated unto His desire, we will end up in a place outside of His will. How often have I seen the desire of men to become something they are not; imitating and franchising the gifts. They are operating in a false anointing that God never issued. I have seen those who prophesy disguised as prophets of God who were never called. Pastors disguised as wolves in sheep clothing can bring destruction into the lives of so many who truly are aspiring for the revelation of truth.

In today's culture, to become a successful pastor can be a lucrative business if you have perfected the talents of man and can speak with a silvery tongue. You can not operate in spiritual things with a religious spirit. Religious things are for man and his kingdom where he anoints himself with the power of man's wisdom to lord over God's creation. He retains all authority unto himself. Spiritual things are for God and His Kingdom with the Saints possessing the power under the authority and rulership of the Holy Spirit. The natural man receives not the things of the Kingdom, only the things that flesh can provide.

> *Indeed you are called a Jew, and rest on the law, and make your boast in God, 18and know His will, and approve the things that are excellent, being instructed out of the law, 19and are confident that you yourself are a guide to the blind, a light to those who are in darkness, 20an instructor of the foolish, a teacher of babes, having the form of knowledge and truth in the law. 21You, therefore, who teach another, do you not teach yourself?* **Romans 2:17-21**

What power do you possess that was not given to you by your Creator? Demonic powers lead men to believe because their name are in lights, the neon signs we see on billboards everywhere, shines brighter than the light of day. Be careful, Lucifer's name means the *"light of day"*. If you are walking in the deception of pride, you can easily pursue a path contending with the will of God. You will end up competing for the praises of men and suffer the judgment of correction. If you are convinced that your name is above

God's name because of the accomplishment of the works of your hands, you have a determined end. *"You will never shine brighter than the light that has already failed; the lesser light that fell from above as lightning that lost its power."* Lucifer's fatal calculation was flawed. He was blinded by his own light not to realize there was a power greater that created him. Pride will blind you! It is an empty agent disguised as a vessel of righteousness. My God daughter calls him *"devil in a three piece suit"*.

Pride is a never ending battle assigned to defeat you. Lucifer's deception was aided by a company of pride, one-third of God's angelic host falling with him. We are to be very vigilant that we do not commit our spiritual energy and resources into the pride of man. It is God's Spirit that will expose the actions in his heart. When we reject the Holy Spirit who keeps us sustained in the grace of God, we have denied the power of the word to be a lamp unto our feet and a light unto our path.

> *O LORD, I know the way of man is not in himself; It is not in man who walks to direct his own steps. 24O LORD, correct me, but with justice; Not in Your anger, lest You bring me to nothing.*
> **Jeremiah 10:23-24**

Chapter 10

 Gone Fishing

Nevertheless, lest we offend them, go to the sea, cast in a hook, and take the fish that comes up first. And when you have opened its mouth, you will find a piece of money; take that and give it to them for Me and you.

Matt. 17:24-27

I have a passion for fishing, particularly deep sea fishing. Besides the experience of venturing into the unknown, there is an ever present hope to capture treasures from the deep. I fish not for recreation alone, but out of necessity to rein in a prize of freshness preserved in the salty aqua waters buried in the fathoms of chance. Fishing is a chance, an opportunity that requires the stillness of patience for success. Even if you have fished all night and caught nothing, the prevailing persistence of chance will motivate you beyond defeat.

Fishing offers moments of relaxation, deep reflections away from the beaten path of the pressings of life into the peace and serenity of quietness. There are no encounters in the deep except for what nature provides; birds hovering overhead; dolphins swimming along side as I am being escorted by the swells of the deep further into the unknown. The deep seems to keep calling me beyond where I've been, reaching further, looking deeper, waiting patiently for the reward of time and chance. Time and chance belongs to us all. The preparation of time seeks the result of faith to connect with destiny.

Our life's journey takes us into unchartered waters, sometimes where others have never been neither desired. Launching out into the deep separates us from our comforts and reference of familiarity that have served us so well. My Mother always said, *"I would rather have tried and failed than never to have tried at all"*. In the community of life, we bond together being our brother's keeper, sharing in their success and failures. Life is not always about winning but loving that transcends any of life's accomplishments.

> *When He had stopped speaking, He said to Simon, "Launch out into the deep and let down your nets for a catch." ⁵But Simon answered and said to Him, "Master, we have toiled all night and caught nothing; nevertheless at Your word I will let down the net." ⁶And when they had done this, they caught a great number of fish, and their net was breaking. ⁷So they signaled to their partners in the other boat to come and help them. And they came and filled both the boats, so that they began to sink.*
> **Luke 5:4-7**

The supreme light of love brings together a union of fellowship as we work to fulfill our destinies. There are times our path will lead us through the *"gate called narrow"* and we must tread alone. It offers *"difficulty in the way but it leads to life and few will find it"*.

I cast my net with the help of those who have also found the way. We fished all night and caught nothing. Then I hear a voice that directs me into the pathway of victory; *"cast your nets on the right side"*. I had been fishing on the wrong side of success with no results. The revelation of Jesus penetrates the depths of the unknown with a word that will shine light to our destination. His Spirit will guide our understanding in the unveiled truth of His knowledge. At the summons of His Word, I became humbled and rendered my obedience to His action of love. However, my obedience was in part to the acceptance of truth. He instructed me to launch into the deep and I did. He told me to let *"down my nets"*; I didn't. I only let down *"one net"!* Past experience dictated my faith in the path of unbelief. The memories of yesterday's failures loomed in the entanglement of my judgment. Our defeats can have a persuasive power on our destiny of faith, if we do not exercise full obedience to the application of His Word.

Goodness and mercy overshadowed my disobedience and offered a reward beyond my denial with abundance sufficient for my needs and the needs of my partners in faith. The lesson learned from the spirit ministered to my unbelief. I acquired an ability to hear accurately with the testimony of obedience which meant more than the materiality of what faith produces.

On another day's voyage into the deep, I hear the voice that says *"leave your net behind, just take your hook"*. It puts a demand on my faith; something I must do alone. The logic of my mind questions because success had been demonstrated using my net after I discovered the right side of faith. What is it that I can catch with a hook that I can't catch with a net? Would not time and chance serve me better using the broad band of strings thrown against the sea of time? But I hear the voice of my conscience; *"the occupation of yesterday's accomplishment does not fulfill the requirement of today's grace"*. The needs of today can only be acquired by the exercising of my faith to present day instruction. What it took in the past justified the sufficiency of that time.

A new day has emerged with greater opportunities and challenges. The veiled darkness of the deep does not yield its treasure so easily even with experience navigating the waters of the unknown. It takes the precision light of revelation to see through what's veiled in darkness to be brought forth in the clarity of light.

"Cast in a hook, and take the fish that comes up first. And when you have opened its mouth, you will find a piece of money."

The design of faith always has a specific destination. It does not conquer all things in its path, only the object it is pursuing. The coordinates of faith released in the instruction of a word targets the success of our efforts to bring a testimony of accuracy. As I applied my obedience, I cast my hook in the murky waters of the unforeseen and connected with the destiny of my instructions. There is a fish; the first fish, that satisfies the pursuit of my faith. I opened its mouth remembering His instructions to find the answer, a piece that is sufficient for my need and His. You don't need all the fish in the sea, just the one equipped with the word.

My initial experience on the mission field took me to Africa. Looking back some 20 years, an indelible testimony still remains with me. I made that journey with a team whose motivations were not all the same. Some went because they were musicians and singers; others went because they were preachers; some went for the approval of man seeking the anointing that was upon another man's life. You know the scripture about Elijah and Elisha how he asked and received a double portion of the anointing. The truth is Elisha was appointed by God to be the successor to Elijah. I have seen the perversion of this truth and manipulation of having you believe that you could receive something that was never meant for you.

> *Also you shall anoint Jehu the son of Nimshi as king over Israel. And Elisha the son of Shaphat of Abel Meholah you shall anoint as prophet in your place.*
> **1 Kings 19:16**

Have you ever asked for a double portion? I did! How vain was I not understanding God's prophetic principles. Looking back at my motives, I was consumed with zeal without understanding. I was guilty of pursuing the gifts, wanting to shine brighter than the light within.

> *My son, if you receive my words, And treasure my commands within you, ²So that you incline your ear to wisdom, And apply your heart to understanding; ³Yes, if you cry out for discernment, And lift up*

your voice for understanding, 4If you seek her as silver, And search for her as hidden treasures; 5Then you will understand the fear of the LORD, And find the knowledge of God. **Proverbs 2:1-5**

Did you ever believe the gifting of man could give you a portion of something that he never had power to do? The anointing comes by divine appointment. If your assignment is as Elisha, you must maintain a commitment and determination to pursue the grace and receive what God has purposed for your life.

And so it was, when they had crossed over, that Elijah said to Elisha, "Ask! What may I do for you, before I am taken away from you?" Elisha said, "Please let a double portion of your spirit be upon me." 10So he said, "You have asked a hard thing. Nevertheless, if you see me when I am taken from you, it shall be so for you; but if not, it shall not be so. **2 Kings 2:9-10**

I was being sent to Africa not fully understanding what God intended to do! Obedience was the only recognizable requirement. We first arrived in Lagos, West Africa. That evening while eating dinner in a restaurant before continuing our journey to Benin, I struck up a conversation with the waiter who was serving me. He told me his name was Ramos. I told the young man who appeared to be around my age that we were having a conference in Benin. I invited him to come and he responded that he would try.

The next morning, we boarded the flight to Benin without him. When we arrived, I was introduced to the people, their culture and their religion. Despite being such an impoverished country, you may not have thought how content and peaceful the people were. I discovered what they did not possess materially, they more than made up for it spiritually. I was introduced to worship and prayer at a level I had not experienced before. There was such an expression of freedom in worship that brought revival to my soul. During this time I was given a prophecy. I was told *"it would take 30 days after I return home to realize why God sent me there"*.

Around the 5th day of the conference, miraculously, Ramos appeared. He said that he did not have a place to stay, so I invited him to stay in the room with me and a friend who was a musician with the praise team. That night, around 10pm, when we retired to my room, I began ministering the word to Ramos. I never had any preoccupation about him neither did I know of his beliefs. I began to discern that he did not understand the words that I was speaking to him. I asked him; are you saved? His response was 'yes'. I recognized that he did not know what he was responding to. At that moment, the spirit of discernment came upon me and I recognized that he had not been saved, baptized or filled with the Holy Ghost. I grabbed his hands as he stood to his feet and began to minister life unto him. As I began to pray, I noticed that his facial demeanor was changing. I began to pray more fervently; praying in the Holy Ghost. The spirit of fear tried to overwhelm me when I saw his face gyrating with contortions and hearing the voices of demons speaking through him. Still holding his hands, I began to pray in a tongue I have never spoken before. It was the tongue of the warring spirit of God elevating above every demonic spirit that had him bound.

After continual prayer until about 3am, Ramos began to experience deliverance. The demonic spirits began to come out of him; ancestral, juju, voodoo, and a complicity of witchcraft that had control over him, left his body. He fell on his knees and began to worship God. Tears of joy rolled down his face. He was free! I collapsed on the bed with all of the anointing drained from me. He had received God's life. When I awoke in the morning, he was prostrated still worshipping God with an endless flow of tears permeating from his spirit. I prayed again with him sealing him in the power of the Holy Ghost. He told me he would never ever forget what he had experienced. His face was glowing; you know the look when the Holy Ghost takes control of your life. It's a look never to be mistaken.

That day, it was noised around the camp meeting the great works that God had done. Ramos came to the sanctuary and testified to the glory of God. Before he left to return to his home, we exchanged information with the promise to keep in touch. Thirty days after my return to the states, I received a letter in the mail. It was Ramos! He told me that he was still grateful for that spiritual encounter. He went on to say upon returning home, God had empowered him to save his family; his father, mother, brothers and sisters. Not only did God save his family, but God had saved his whole village from the powers of juju. He went further to say that God had called him into the ministry! Glory to God! He asked for my help. You would think he wanted money; NO! He asked for books, bibles; only the things needed to sustain spiritual growth and development. A spiritual hunger had arisen within him; an unquenchable thirst for the living waters.

The prophecy I had received had come true; 30 days! The revelation of the *"one hook and the first fish"* still inspires me even until this day. Jesus will teach you how to become a fisher of men. The only requirement of faith is an obedience and willingness to pursue the will of God.

God requires our obedience and availability to manifest His Kingdom. If you would dare but ask, *"Here I am Lord, send me"*. Or is your life so important to yourself full of commitments to man, material things and a dependency on people that will not afford you the opportunity to experience surfing in the deeper waters of faith.

It is always miraculous when God meets us in a place where we least expect it and unpredictably manifest Himself in dimensions that we have no reference to any prior encounters with Him. Remember Moses and the burning bush? It speaks of spiritual revelation beyond human comprehension. The anointings of God are beyond any natural predictability.

> And the Angel of the LORD appeared to him in a flame of fire from the midst of a bush. So he looked, and behold, the bush was burning with fire, but the bush was not consumed. ³Then Moses said, "I will now turn aside and see this great sight, why the bush does not burn." ⁴So when the LORD

saw that he turned aside to look, God called to him from the midst of the bush and said, Moses, Moses!" And he said, "Here I am". **Exodus 3:2-4**

Moses saw the fire. His natural abilities could discern the burning of the bush, but he did not have the spiritual sight to see the Angel that was being revealed to him from the midst of the bush. Neither could he discern the ground that he was standing on. When you are standing on God's ground, Holy Ground, there should be nothing that separates you from His presence. Take off your shoes and encounter the revelation of the moment. You will never see the revelation of God dealing with peripheral things neither will you be able to comprehend spiritual things with the natural talents of man.

Our level of spiritual gifting varies from one to the other but of the same spirit. Moses could not see, but he could hear. Even though he did not have spiritual sight, he had a spiritual ear to hear the voice of God. He responded, *"Here I am!"* It was only when God removed His garment of light that Moses realized that he had entered the realm of the Lord's habitation. Despite our gifting, what is consistent in the life of every believer is an ability to hear the voice of God even in the seclusion of a wilderness or the rumbling of earthquakes. Without ears to hear, we have no voice to speak.

> *But the natural man does not receive the things of the Spirit of God, for they are foolishness to him; nor can he know them, because they are spiritually discerned.*
> **1 Cor. 2:14**

Power of Light

Do you realize the power of light? Light makes things invisible and transparent, but it also reveals. The power of light even has the ability to disclose things hiding in the dark. We sometimes associate darkness as a place of evil; not necessarily so. It could be for your own good that what's hidden in the dark is not discovered until God's timing is unveiled. The revelation of things too early can have an affect on your obedience. Faith operates in the blind by not knowing the end from the beginning.

There are those who operate in the shadow of light who are only able to produce diminished results, forecasting the future without the knowledge the fullness of light reveals. Faith is the light of our future empowering us with sight to navigate the path of the unknown. It has its own energy fueled by the power of our prayers. Strengthened with confidence and boldness, faith catapults with speed as Elijah running before the rains.

We can see light with our natural senses but never beyond it. It is incredible to realize that our natural minds are equipped to think at the speed of 186,000mps; the realm of seen things. The speed of light is the parameter that separates visible from invisible realities. Revelation is a dimension beyond the speed of light. To get there requires an acceleration of God's energy that we come to know as vision. When we move beyond the speed of light the unseen becomes seen; invisibility takes on the form of recognition.

"He that hears the word and does not understand risk the chance of it being snatched away." Just as the sun rises to bring light to the things God reveals, it also sets and

darkness emerges to cast shadows over truth. We must never forget in the pressings of the dark what was revealed in the light. If we are to advance into the greater dimensions of what God intends to perform in our times, we must do more than hear. We must receive His deposits into good ground (fallowed ground) if we expect the increase.

> *But he that received seed into the good ground is he that heareth the word, and understandeth it; which also beareth fruit, and bringeth forth, some an hundredfold, some sixty, some thirty.* **Matt. 13:23**

Chapter 11

Fallow Ground

For thus says the LORD to the men of Judah and Jerusalem: "Break up your fallow ground, And do not sow among thorns.
Jeremiah 4:3

Whathat does it mean to fallow? *"The tilling of land without sowing it for a season; cultivated land that is allowed to lie idle during the growing season."* Fallowing is a process of preparation necessary for enlargement. God desires to increase in our lives beyond measure into the manifold proportions of His grace. The responsibility of preparation is solely ours and it must be fulfilled before the resources necessary for our destiny are released. Preparation fulfills the requirement for increase.

Often times we read and study the word out of necessity and obligation. But the opportunity of the pure moments of interacting with God through His word to discover His grace eludes us. The revelation of His heart requires diligence seeking beyond the veil of what is written. The discovery of revelation in past visitations occupies the demands for our teaching and preaching. But do we search the scriptures to find His love and our place of destiny that can only be revealed in His presence. The revealing power of the word is beyond any factual application. At the instance of our encounter with Him, He will overwhelm our hearts with words specific to our destiny. I have spent years writing the word upon the tablets of my memory; chapter by chapter, verse by verse. But what was written did not possess the power of fulfillment until the Spirit interacted with my confessions to bring life to my diligence. The word of the Lord says *"I sent my word to heal thee"*. The word is true but it must become specific as an answer to our prayer. When God hears and honors our prayer, the life of what is written will manifest a performance that only the Holy Spirit can enact. A word deposited in the womb of faith will become flesh when the power of God's Spirit is released to bring a testimony of His faithfulness. When we fallow the channels to heaven's resources, we will have opened a pathway for the delivery of answers to our prayers.

Patience

Fallowing is a process that requires patience. Patience must be developed in ourselves, patience with others, and patience with God. Often times we fail in the test of endurance because of the requirement of waiting. God is not a magician; He is a God of miracles. Daniel fasted and prayed with sackcloth and ashes before the Angel Gabriel responded to his prayer. It took twenty one days from the time of his prayer to receive an answer. Our answers don't always come so speedily. Persistence in prayer involves patience and waiting that often test our faith. If we believe to see the result of our faith, we will wait for the revealing of our confidence.

In this you greatly rejoice, though now for a little while, if need be, you have been grieved by various trials, ⁷that the genuineness of your faith, being much more precious than gold that perishes, though it is tested by fire, may be found to praise, honor, and glory at the revelation of Jesus Christ, ⁸whom having not seen you love. Though now you do not see Him, yet believing, you rejoice with joy inexpressible and full of glory. **1 Peter 1:6-8**

Have you considered how a pearl is made? Firstly, it is a process and sometimes it can be a long process. A pearl is not developed without some type of irritant.

"A pearl is formed when an organic parasite penetrates the shell of a mollusk and lodges in its soft inner body. Upon penetrating the shell the parasite encounters cells within the mollusk's mantle tissue and these cells grow into a sac which envelops the intruder. This sac is known as a pearl sac which begin excreting a chemical substance of nacre."

Just as the formation of the pearl, the life of the Believer can not grow without the trials of life that is purposed for the proving of faith. We are attacked from all sides by the parasites of this world that become illegal attachments not purposed for our destiny. They are no more than leeches sent to drain us of our spiritual substance. The plan is to deny us the essence of God's life; *"the blood of Jesus"*. It is the blood that sustains the God life the leeches feast upon.

The leech has two daughters, Give and Give! There are three things that are never satisfied, Four never say, "Enough!" 16The grave, The barren womb, The earth that is not satisfied with water, And the fire never says, "Enough!" **Proverbs 30:15-16**

If we are bound in unity to defend in prayer, we will cancel every assignment of any intruding force that comes against us. Without development of a prayer life sufficient for warfare, we will fail in our ability to access the power center of our faith. The consequence will leave us in an anemic state with no power to defend. Prayer and faith are constants of our warfare.

We are encased by the protective shell of the anointing, sealed with the power of the Holy Spirit. But, if we are not diligent in our cooperation with the guidance that God's anointing provides, just like the mollusk, our fabric will be penetrated and our mantle will suffer compromise. We are a body and the members of the body stand as one when confronted with the enemy's aggression. We must stand against the powers of disobedience, unbelief and fear. When discernment of our atmosphere detects an intruder, the intruder will be enveloped by a protective hedge, a sac that forms a shield around it, and destroyed by the saving prayer of faith.

Above all, taking the shield of faith with which you will be able to quench all the fiery darts of the wicked one.
Ephesians 6:16

If the greater is to emerge out of our struggles, the patience of the collective body will be tested. Just as the pearl, when our mantle suffers exposure to the enemy (the mantle of righteousness), it produces an opportunity for the strength of our unity of shielded faith to defend and avenge the aggression of fiery darts. We come together to form a bond of unity, defending the grace, embracing a cooperate anointing that excretes and grows into something greater. *"The more we are afflicted, the more we grow."*

Be reminded that we are a body and the body exists above our individual spiritual altitude and exploits. There is no one entity who is all of who God called us to be. We are the full embodiment of Christ here on earth.

> *There is one body, and one Spirit, even as ye are called in one hope of your calling; ⁵One Lord, one faith, one baptism, ⁶One God and Father of all, who is above all, and through all, and in you all.* **Ephesians 4:4-6**

Prepare Yourself

> *Prepare your outside work, Make it fit for yourself in the field; And afterward build your house.* **Psalms 24:27**

Preparation is part of the requirement to fulfill the prophetic instructions that are given to us to carry out. Without a clear understanding of our purpose, our time of development can be a lengthy process. The management of our priorities will become essential to fulfilling our destiny. When the season of opportunity arises, we must have completed the process of our outside work to advance into the next level. Preparation precedes our availability at the time the Lord intends to use us.

> *Therefore prepare yourself and arise, And speak to them all that I command you. Do not be dismayed before their faces, Lest I dismay you before them.* **Jeremiah 1:17**

Prepare yourself, then arise and speak what you are commanded to say! In 2005, I received a mandate to return to Africa. Through God's orchestration, I journeyed to the country of Ghana, West Africa. I began the work by preaching the Gospel throughout the country. I worked with reckless abandonment carrying out the call of God. There were many churches that joined together to bring reconciliation and healing to a new generation of Believers. We established the ministry of Emerging Destiny in Accra, Ghana. Through much warfare and perseverance, a vibrant spiritual organism emerged that continues to bring reconciliation to the Body of Christ.

I discerned as I traveled extensively throughout the country that much had been done to evangelize the territory. Sadly to admit, they were left at the watering hole of perplexity. It left a void in my spirit as I began to travail how the people were left to fend for themselves. There have been many that have gone before me and flooded the land with much religion and tradition. There is a responsibility we have as Believers to reach the world delivering the fullness of the gospel. Jesus always delivered a balanced diet to the hungry. He fed the multitude naturally and spiritually with the abundance of miraculous grace.

I admit Africa offers unique challenges of culture and dialect. There is a level of patience required because of the cultural differences. Patience takes time and compassion will linger if we are to deliver the fullness of our assignment. However, as I traveled throughout the land, I discerned that Africa had only received a portion, the works of evangelism. The establishment of true ministry was done in part. Where were all the ministry gifts that were so badly needed to build a true and strong foundation? Did we count the cost of our commitment to steward the people of God? For the most part, we left them in the wilderness of John the Baptist. We took them down to the Jordan, dipped them in the pool but did not walk with them through the fire. We were faithful in our commitment to baptize them, but we fell short in our efforts to patiently develop them through their trials and tribulations. In their thirst and hunger, we left the door open that nullified much of the progress that we worked so hard to accomplish. Jesus said we ought to fulfill the whole law. Good done in part can be worst than any good at all. It can be seen as a betrayal.

> *A brother offended is harder to win than a strong city, and contentions are like the bars of a castle.* **Proverbs 18:19**

It is very difficult to continue in an environment where there are strong contentions rooted in betrayal. The reason we are in Afghanistan today is because of a betrayal where we committed ourselves to do something that we neglected to do. Once an ally fighting in battle together, we promised to help them rebuild their country, but we never did.

Sounds like some of our churches today committing to help in our communities to improve the lives of the people but after their participation in establishing our ministries, we leave them there. We stand in their midst erecting our churches and building monuments of our accomplishments but never giving back while continuing to drain the resources from the community. If there is no profit or gain, we have no need even though we say we are non-profit. We will redo our analysis and move to an area that will sustain us in our pursuits. Our success is never to be measured in the ability of our hands but by the requirement of obedience woven into our instructions. An accurate interpretation of God's instructions and the application of our obedience will reap the rewards of goodness and mercy.

> *Sow for yourselves righteousness; Reap in mercy; Break up your fallow ground, "For it is time to seek the LORD", Till He comes and rains righteousness on you.*
> **Hosea 10:12**

We have an awesome level of responsibility when God commands us to "do" something, despite how uncommon it may be. Doing is an indication of our level of obedience to divine instructions. It is key to the discovery of God's grace if we are to have an encounter with Him. We are commanded to perform His Word according to all that He instructs us to do.

> *"Ah, Lord GOD! Behold, I cannot speak, for I am a youth." 7But the LORD said to me: "Do not say, 'I am a youth,' For you*

shall go to all to whom I send you, And whatever I command you, you shall speak. 8Do not be afraid of their faces, For I am with you to deliver you," says the LORD. **Jeremiah 1:6-8**

Ministry is not determined by our natural abilities. If we have a dependency on our self-will to perform the things of the Kingdom, we will fail. The gifts of God are instruments purposed to be used by the Holy Spirit to carry out the performances of faith. Our talents are no substitute for His ability. When we learn to take self out of the equation and extrapolate the depths of faith, we will realize that "it is not by our might nor by our power but by God's Spirit".

And the man said to me, "Son of man, look with your eyes and hear with your ears, and fix your mind on everything I show you; for you were brought here so that I might show them to you. Declare to the house of Israel everything you see". **Ezekiel 40:4**

Obedience is the Exercising of Faith

Obedience is the key to a divine encounter with God. After He releases His instructions, we then must exercise faith as an indication of our cooperation with Him which is purposed to produce a greater measure of His glory. The action of our faith opens the window to greater revelations where he intends to *"show us more things to come"*. God has promised that he would "open the windows of heaven to give us an advancing of His glory". The greater our obedience, the greater the persecution, the greater the revelation!

That the trial of your faith, being much more precious than of gold that perisheth, though it be tried with fire, might be found unto praise and honour and glory at the appearing of Jesus Christ: Whom having not seen, ye love; in whom now ye see him not yet believing, ye rejoice with joy unspeakable and full of glory: "Receiving the end of your faith, even the salvation of your souls. **1 Peter 1:7-9**

Fan the Flame

The ultimate lesson of obedience comes from the testimony of Adam in the garden of God's creation. I have been searching for the *"Garden of Eden"* for quite some time. It may seem rather ridiculous to search for something that does not exist. What I am able to ascertain has been an error of our teaching. We make assumptions and establish a truth based on the error of our reasoning. For example, there are those who still believe that Eve ate an apple! Where did that come from? Was that the forbidden fruit?

The LORD God planted a garden eastward in Eden, and there He put the man whom He had formed. **Genesis 2:8**

In the Garden of the Lord, Adam was given the responsibility to *"tend and guard"* the things of the Lord's creation. He was to provide a covering that would complete God's plan to be a protector of all that was delegated to him. He was instructed to tend, cultivate with the intent to yield an increase and expand with the multiplicity of his gifts to reproduce the image of God's creation. His instructions were simple; maintain the order that God had established. As a king of his domain governing the affairs of God's newly created Kingdom, Adam also had the responsibility to guard, create a protective hedge against every intrusive spirit. He had a free will spirit to pursue the desires of his choice except for the forbidden. In the center of his habitation was the forbidden and a command to not violate the law of his occupation. He had legal rights and authority over everything contained within except the *"tree of good and evil"* that coexisted with the *"tree of life"*.

The Garden was a place of living in the presence of the Lord. In the shared responsibility of fulfilling God's instructions with his newly acquired help, Adam enjoyed the security and love that would last forever. There was no need for him to seek revelation outside of his dwelling place. He only had to look around and see the revelation that was before him of an everlasting Kingdom. He lived in a place consumed with daily communion experiencing the Lord's presence. His daily grace was satisfied in his obedience.

When Adam was alone, before the presentation of the woman made from his bone, he had the responsibility all to himself. When his help came, he assumed the position of delegating his responsibility. The power of authority possessed in one's hand does not equate to delegated power given to someone else. They are on two different levels. Authority rested in the hands of Adam and not the one who he delegated responsibility. When the serpent appeared, maybe Adam did not exercise sound judgment tending when he should have been guarding; *"guarding what God had given him including his help"*. It can be perceived Adam was fulfilling His ministry of Love, the sacred life of obedience, while the lesser part of his judgment rendered an authority of her own.

We must recognize, those that are joined to us can be entertaining things outside the realm of God's acceptance while we remain in pursuit of an obedient life. Adam's help became distracted from the life of obedience by the seductive power of distraction. She was deceived by the enemy but Adam, the one with the ultimate authority was presented with a clear and painful choice. If we are not careful, we can be caught up in a life of disobedience by the choices that others present to us. The consequence of error can lead into judgment and rejection of God's vision for our lives. We must live above excuses and separate the failures of others who are joined to us. Truth is an absolute that requires an obedience to match.

The fire of eternity at the core of man's heart was extinguished when sin prevailed over the good conscience of righteousness. Man lost his authority to rule and now has become dependent upon *"the ability to hear"* for direction back to the place where he was separated from. The violation of God's righteousness produces sin and exposes our nakedness in defeat. The choice of our obedience is ever before us. We have the power to choose life and live within the constraints of God's righteousness or suffer the penalty of a divided choice between good and evil. If we do not discriminate between the good conscience of righteousness and the choices that others present to us, we never will experience the law of grace that frees us from the choice of good and evil.

Chapter 12

Lord, I Have a Question

If you have run with the footmen, and they have wearied you, Then how can you contend with horses? And if in the land of peace, In which you trusted, they wearied you, Then how will you do in the floodplain of the Jordan? **Jeremiah 12:5**

Have you ever experienced an onslaught of attacks from the enemy who had purposed in his heart to destroy you? Did you *"walk through the valley of the shadow of death intimidated by fear"?* Did you walk and not run or did you have a panic attack when the fear of evil overwhelmed your heart? What was your testimony? Did you reveal your cause to the righteous judge? I assume your spiritual senses awoke to discover the protective grace the Lord provides and His power to deliver. I have been there! I cried out from deep within, *"Lord, let not mine enemy triumph over me"!*

The Prophet Jeremiah, just a teenager at the age of seventeen, was confronted with a similar battle. The lack of maturity is forgiving, to be young and stupid is another; but to be old and stupid is irrevocable. Oops! Sorry. Jeremiah's initial complaint was concerning spiritual deception; why didn't he know what God knew of the devised schemes being perpetrated against him that were meant to destroy him? Jeremiah said *"I was like a docile lamb brought to the slaughter"*. At the root of Jeremiah's problem was the fear of what man could do to him. God had previously given Jeremiah His instructions when He first called him; *"do not look at their faces. I am with you to deliver you"*.

Faces have power to speak and can be intimidating. Looks are deceptive portrayals designed to disguise the heart, but they also reveal what lies beneath the surface of our smiles. We have to be careful; looks are joined with the spirit of familiarity purposed to illegally penetrate into our secret places revealing things about us that we have guarded so well. The judging of looks can also lead to a wrong conclusion based on perception without spiritual discernment. My Mother taught us not to be quick to judge because it is the power of the Holy Spirit operating in our lives that is the judge of all things seen and unseen.

Fear is a process that develops in the heart as a consequential result where faith and trust has lost the battle to rule. Fear has no power of its own and must be fed by the power of unbelief which denies access to truth. Unbelief and fear are very disfiguring. Together, they disfigure and rearrange the images of God's creation within you; wounded with stains of defeat. Subsequently, you will see yourself differently; no royal priesthood, no knight in shining armour but the raised flag of surrender of the defeated. You will become something other than who God intended because you lack the courage; eliminating the possibility of escape. I can guarantee you will not like what you see. Self hatred and pity will settle in your inner man because of an inability to overcome. You will become mesmerized and focused on the failures that hold you bound with no vision of success rather than the possibilities of life that faith renders.

Love is pure and has power to heal the wounds of defeat. The light of love shines deep bringing light to the areas of darkness suppressed by our fears. Fear in the presence of light attempts to retreat but it cannot hide. It is then faith emerges. I have a God given solution for fear; Love yourself, love yourself to believe. Believe your way out. Grab a hold of the promises of God and keep them ever before you. Faith bears the testimony of Christ. If you want to learn faith, *"defeat the power of your unbelief and faith will emerge"*. Faith is a conqueror! By faith are you saved; it is the gift of God. Faith will sustain you in your struggles if you *"receive and believe the word"*.

Faith is an action that attaches to our belief to perform the *"works of faith"*. It has a direct link to our gifts which are empowered by the Holy Spirit to accomplish the *"work of our ministry"*. We all have a ministry and it is the ministry of love. If the supremacy of Christ dwells within, faith will emerge to perform what you have accepted. Believe it, receive it! Jesus had faith to believe in the resurrection and that power remains within us. The battle of faith that is won in our hearts gives us power to live above defeat and fear. We should never put a dependency on ourselves to do what faith is purposed to do. The natural man does not understand things concerning the spiritual. We can not perform spiritual functions with the limitations of our hands gloved in the inequity of pride.

Jeremiah gave indication of his dissatisfaction of being left in the dark when God opened his eyes to the enemy's plans. Our mantle will be tested by every possible imagination of the adversary and his allies. We can never anticipate or know the motives hidden in the heart of man unless the Holy Spirit brings revelation that exposes the enemy's deceptions. Sometimes in our warfare, fear will surface and we forget what we are called to do, which can negate the power of the mantle that rests upon us. Jeremiah realized that God was testing his mind and the secret things of his heart.

> *But, O LORD of hosts, You who judge righteously, Testing the mind and the heart, Let me see Your vengeance on them, For to You I have revealed my cause.*
> **Jeremiah 11:20**

In the midst of all our battles, we will be tested. Our character and integrity will be measured by the standard of the word that the Lord has given us. This is an opportunity for the development of our faith. If we are not strong, we will waver in the things we say we believe. We have developed elaborate skills to mask our failures with the power of our self- righteousness. Show me a person who is self-righteous and I will show you a person who suffers from the fear of failure. Pride will defend your defeats and mask the weakness of your heart. Vindictiveness is an agent of pride that attempts to retaliate against exposure. It is malicious in intent and motivated by spite that lacks the power of forgiveness. Sadly to say, vindictiveness is the end process of resentment that has been harbored in the heart beyond reconciliation of remorse.

Just as fear is an action of unbelief, faith is an action of a heart centered in belief. God honors the actions of our faith by defending His word to establish truth. Faith united with the actions of His Spirit will bring confirmation of His word as a testimony of truth.

The Lord responded to Jeremiah's request and issued His judgment to avenge His word and honor the promise He had given; *"to deliver him"*.

> *Therefore thus says the LORD concerning the men of Anathoth who seek your life, saying, 'Do not prophesy in the name of the LORD, lest you die by our hand'* ^{22}*therefore thus says the LORD of hosts: 'Behold, I will punish them. The young men shall die by the sword, their sons and their daughters shall die by famine;* ^{23}*and there shall be no remnant of them, for I will bring catastrophe on the men of Anathoth, even the year of their punishment.'*
> **Jeremiah 11:21-23**

You would have expected that Jeremiah would have expressed genuine gratitude for the Lord's faithfulness, without complaint. But this was not to be the case. Why question God when he has chosen to work things out for your good? What more should you expect beyond what grace provides? It was not enough for Jeremiah that God said he would bring catastrophe on his enemies. He still had questions. Why am I still fighting this battle when you have power to end it right now?

Righteous are You, O LORD, when I plead with You; Yet let me talk with You about Your judgments. Why does the way of the wicked prosper? Why are those happy who deal so treacherously? ²You have planted them, yes, they have taken root; They grow, yes, they bear fruit. You are near in their mouth But far from their mind. ³But You, O LORD, know me; You have seen me, And You have tested my heart toward You. Pull them out like sheep for the slaughter, And prepare them for the day of slaughter. ⁴How long will the land mourn, And the herbs of every field wither? The beasts and birds are consumed, For the wickedness of those who dwell there, Because they said, "He will not see our final end." **Jeremiah 12:1-4**

What prevails in the heart of man that he should question the sovereignty of the judgments of the Lord? Is it an effort to change the outcome that was seen from the beginning? To accept that premise means you know the outcome of the future. Or are you in disagreement and would have judged it another way? Was it zeal; being moved by compassion for the suffering and persecution of your generation? Scripture says it is a terrible thing to be turned over to the judgments of man. "If the rulers of this age had known the consequence of the cross, they never would have crucified the Lord of Glory."

We are in the middle of the Lord's battle and we are to carry out His instructions to fulfill His vision. He knows the beginning and end of all things. The heart of man lacks the depth of compassion and love to be trusted to judge. Our solutions are not God's solutions. Our powers are limited. We are not equipped to separate good from evil, right from wrong, hope from defeat. We will lose the wheat trying to separate the chaff.

Some of you may say Jeremiah was complaining, fearful, and quite frankly arrogant. In my earlier years, I was accused of being a *"wild buck"*. I never felt the threat of man but man felt the threat of the revelations that were in me. Man made the mistake of judging from the outside but never knew the secret life I had with God in my prayer closet. The open display of what is accomplished in the dark will always bring a confrontation to the powers that are intimidated by spiritual revelation. The brilliance of the light of revelation out shines the lights of past knowledge.

There is something about the testimony of Jeremiah's complaint that gives indication of his relationship with the Lord. Jeremiah was trusted enough that regardless of what his contentions may have been, He knew the love of God that would hear the *"cry of his voice"*. We can learn from his level of transparency and honesty, however skewed it may have been. He spoke from the reservoir of his contentions and they were many. There is a lesson to learn: *"Speak what is on your mind and do not harbor in your heart the carryings of your indecisions"*. Seek an answer. If you are not quick to do that, vexation and wrath will take root and cause turmoil in your life. It is easier to fix the error of your thinking than to find solutions in the midst of confusion. Remember that *"a wise man will hear and increase in learning and a man of good understanding shall attain unto wise counsel"*. Self-righteousness in the heart of man is very dangerous. It will not produce God's result. All men possess the imperfection of righteousness and are not meant to judge pertaining to the Lord's judgments.

Success and defeat are determined by our level of patience. Waiting creates a conduit to apprehend the revelations of God. He will reveal His supremacy as He chooses. He will raise one and put down the other. Our victories will only be achieved when we are rested in His judgments and His power to perform His word. If we are not able to understand the purpose and intent of His judgments, we will question the results based on our perception of what we believe should be the consequences of His actions. God's thoughts are not our thoughts and it would behoove us to wait on His revelations for an understanding of His intentions. There will always be a level of dissatisfaction amongst the discontent of how He has chosen to render His grace, mercy and judgments, but *"Father knows best"*.

It was revealed to Jeremiah that his future would not be any easier; times would be harder with greater challenges. He was being launched from the little leagues into a world of big contenders. If we are truly committed, the actualizing of our faith level will lead us into greater battles beyond any reference of past experiences. *"If you have been running with the footmen and you have gotten weary, what will you do when the horses comes."*

In our battles, we all at some point will suffer weariness. Weariness is not a negative thing, but worry is! Worry attacks your faith and makes you apprehensive which is purposed to keep you out of the battle, but weariness is a confirmation of your efforts, your struggles to endure through your journey. *"Do not get weary in well doing, but be strong and of good faith and realize your reward."* Keep it visualized before you. Scripture says that even Jesus became weary but he never worried. When weariness settled in, He did what we all should do, *"sit"*. If you are of the mind set that you can do everything all by yourself, *"you will fall asleep"*. Some years ago I heard a man of God say *"find rest before rest finds you"*.

> *Now Jacob's well was there. Jesus therefore, being wearied from His journey, sat thus by the well. It was about the sixth hour. ⁷A woman of Samaria came to draw water. Jesus said to her, "Give Me a drink." ⁸For His disciples had gone away into the city to buy food.* **John 4:6-8**

Jesus wearied on His journey became thirsty but His disciples had went away into the city to buy food. Jesus was resting while His disciples were somewhere eating! Weariness is a spiritual place, a temporary place meant for refreshing; reinvigorating our strength to continue. Tiredness comes from the exertion of physical energy and the only recovery from that is sleep. Fulfillment of our purpose can not be completed without the replenishing of our faith. Our spiritual pursuits will often lead us in the path that can be long and enduring. Our physical and spiritual strength will drain if our lives are committed to bringing empowerment to those we encounter. With a constant demand from touching, feeling, pulling and the power of our impartations require that we maintain a constant reservoir of strength.

Weariness created an opportunity for Jesus to give life to the woman that He met at the well in Samaria. He was able to bring her into the true life of living waters. As I was reading this passage, I became amazed at the spiritual economy of Christ. Jesus' mission was for Samaria but He had a need away from the beaten path.

> He left Judea and departed again to Galilee. ⁴But He needed to go through Samaria. **John 4:3-4**

What is so compelling that motivates you to go where you go? Is it an attempt to connect with destiny by the instructions of faith off the beaten path where others have not been? Or are you treading the path of familiarity in pursuit of your ambitions beyond where the instructions of faith are taking you? Scripture says clearly that Jesus had *"need to go through Samaria"*. However, because of His weariness, He came to a well on the out skirts of Sychar near a plot of land that Jacob gave to his son Joseph.

The Samaritan woman had a divine appointment with Jesus. She experienced the revelation that *"He was the fountain of living water springing up into everlasting life"*.

> The woman then left her waterpot, went her way into the city, and said to the men, ²⁹"Come, see a Man who told me all things that I ever did. Could this be the Christ?" ³⁰Then they went out of the city and came to Him. **John 4:28-30**

What is so remarkable concerning this passage is the transforming power of Christ that will alter your path. Jesus impacted the life of the Samaritan woman and made her a witness for Him. She came to the well to fetch water, but she left her water pot in exchange to carry the testimony of Jesus. The power that testified even in His weariness resulted in; *"they went out of the city and came to HIM"*. The testimony of one woman impacted a nation.

> *Then they said to the woman, "Now we believe, not because of what you said, for we ourselves have heard Him and we know that this is indeed the Christ, the Savior of the world."* **John 4:42**

> *Therefore the disciples said to one another, Has anyone brought Him anything to eat?"* ³⁴*Jesus said to them, My food is to do the will of Him who sent Me, and to finish His work.* **John 4:33-34**

The disciples of Jesus went away into the city to buy food. They had the same opportunity as the Samaritan woman to deliver the testimony of Jesus. The pursuit of faith will reveal the true motives and ambitions that lie in a man's heart. It is not always that people are truly connected to your need, passion and vision. Some ally with you in deception promoting their own interest until they have extracted from your influence all that you have to give. When the bonds of connectivity are tested, time will bring revelation to what was originally conceived in their heart. I have seen the motivations of men and their priorities attached themselves to the anointing of others in pursuit of their own advancement. Why did the disciples leave Jesus alone to fend for Himself? Their concern was about their own interest; their own provisions.

Familiarity

Those that are closely connected to you will develop a level of familiarity. Familiarity will breed contempt. The arena of contempt is flooded with competition; competition to compete with you, replace you or rise above you.

> Now after two days he departed thence, and went into Galilee. For Jesus Himself testified, that a prophet hath no honour in his own country. Then when he was come into Galilee, the Galilaeans received him, having seen all the things that he did at Jerusalem at the feast: for they also went unto the feast. So Jesus came again into Cana of Galilee, where he made the water wine. **John 4:43-46**

There is no better example of familiarity and contempt than that which compares to the life of a prophet. It is very difficult for a prophet, one who is being sent with a prophetic mandate, to establish God's order where the spirit of familiarity prevails. It takes separation from the environments of familiarity to be an independent voice to proclaim the things of the Spirit. Jesus was from Nazareth but they received Him in Galilee because of the manifestation of the anointing they had seen in Jerusalem. It is interesting to note that Jesus performed His first miracle in Cana, the place where He is now returning to; where He turned "water into wine". We as believers must develop a depth in our prayer life that takes natural things that God has already given us and turn them into a supernatural expansion of His grace. However, what was manifested at the feast in Jerusalem bared a greater significance than the beginning of His miracles in Cana. Scriptures records:

> *And they believed the scripture, and the word which Jesus had said. Now when he was in Jerusalem at the Passover, in the feast day, many believed in his name, when they saw the miracles which he did. But Jesus did not commit himself unto them, because he knew all men, And needed not that any should testify of man: for he knew what was in man.*
> **John 2:22-25**

They believed the scripture and the word which Jesus spoke. As prophetic people, we must accept those things that God says as truth regardless of the vehicle that He uses to communicate His desire. This was the source of Jesus' rejection in Galilee. From a traditional perspective, it may seem more convenient to accept the testimonies written on tablets of stone more than it is to accept the revelations revealed by the Holy Spirit. It takes the discerning ear of the Holy Spirit to translate truth. The Bible says that *"scriptures were written by Holy men of old being moved by the inspiration of the Holy Ghost"*. What they recorded were revelations revealed by the Spirit of the Living God. I know that scripture ends with the book of Revelation, but somebody needs to hear this: *"God has not stopped talking and neither should you to the command of His voice."*

Just because you can not see gravity does not mean that it does not exist neither because of your inability to hear the voice of the Spirit of Christ does not authenticate your doctrine of unbelief. If we accept past truths written by Holy Men of Old as they were moved by the Spirit, it would be considered hypocrisy to reject the revelations that the Holy Spirit reveals in prophesy.

I remember as a child hearing the Saints sing *"I am going to lay down my burdens, down by the riverside, I ain't going to study war no more"*. We have studied long enough. It is time to enter the battle laying aside our waiting and confront the Goliath of our time. Let us move forward, not leaving revelation past but reaching toward the future.

> *Then Balaam answered and said to the servants of Balak, "Though Balak were to give me his house full of silver and gold, I could not go beyond the word of the LORD my God, to do less or more.*
> **Numbers 22:18**

Prior to God visiting Moses on Mount Sinai, there had been no revelation recorded of His past performances. Moses encountered Him on top of Mount Sinai and was given the first 5 books of the Bible, the Pentateuch. We all accept that as truth which has given us the foundation of our belief. The prophetic record that is documented in scripture speaks of God's past performances, present day truth and His intent in the future. We have accepted those things that are *"written as learning"*. We must also accept God's prophetic voice that speaks into our future.

The preparation and accomplishments of our faith should create spiritual opportunities for the Lord to use us. Our spiritual growth is dependent upon our obedience and attitudes. God told Moses to speak to the rock, but what did he do; he struck the rock. We have to develop an attitude that is consistent with our faith. As a child, when we were given instructions and our attitude reflected discontent, we suffered the consequence of correction. The correction was only for the purpose of discipline in the development of skills necessary for the challenges ahead.

Our attitude will in fact determine our altitude. Attitude is a reflection of our level of willingness and confidence in our ability to perfect the things that are delegated to us. Without a willing heart committed to obedience, we will fail in every attempt to accomplish what we set out to do. Our attitudes can be either positive or negative.

Our feelings have a tendency to shape the attitudes we apply to our judgments that will affect the decisions we make. Feelings can be very difficult to contend with because of the inconsistency of our emotions. They are transient, constantly fluctuating above and below our threshold. Our feelings are to remain tempered, seasoned with the consistency of grace and experience. This was Jeremiah's problem; allowing his feelings to interfere with his destiny. Often times they get in the way and can shorten our destiny of hope. Our feelings and emotions are predictably unstable. Out of control, they will raise havoc in our lives.

If our feelings are not protected and our emotions guarded, our passions will become unstable and darken our understanding beyond the reach of love. When love becomes alienated from our conscience, we will have committed to a life of ignorance. This process will lead us to *"being past feeling"*, a hardening of heart not affected by the things around us. It is a dreadful life with the calloused of conscience; a life that is completely consumed in unrighteousness. Love and compassion gives immunity to our heart felt feelings and provides a covering of perpetual peace.

Chapter 13

Restoring the Office of the Deacon

Therefore, brethren, seek out from among you seven men of good reputation, full of the Holy Spirit and wisdom, whom we may appoint over this business; ⁴but we will give ourselves continually to prayer and to the ministry of the word." ⁵And the saying pleased the whole multitude. And they chose Stephen, a man full of faith and the Holy Spirit, and Philip, Prochorus, Nicanor, Timon, Parmenas, and Nicolas, a proselyte from Antioch, ⁶whom they set before the apostles; and when they had prayed, they laid hands on them. ⁷Then the word of God spread, and the number of the disciples multiplied greatly in Jerusalem, and a great many of the priests were obedient to the faith. ⁸And Stephen, full of faith and power, did great wonders and signs among the people. **Acts 6:3-8**

Some of you may wonder what does the office of the deacon have to do with apostolic restoration. The most neglected spiritual ordained office in the Body of Christ is that of the 'Deacon'. Jesus set apart His Apostles; the Apostles set apart Deacons. Scripture gives us a glimpse into the lives of those who were set apart to serve as deacons; consecrated by prayer, men of good reputation, men full of the Holy Spirit and wisdom and separated with the laying on of hands by the Apostles. I would like to refer to the Deacon as the mature saint; men full of the anointing and the wisdom of God called to be servants in the Body of Christ. Men of faith are necessary in maturing the Body into the fullness of God's intended purpose.

As I look at the testimony of Stephen, I make mention of him as one of God's exceptions. Scripture says that not only was Stephen full of the anointing but he was anointed with power by the Holy Spirit to perform above the expectation of what he was required to do. His faith drove him beyond serving men to perform mighty exploits to the men that he served. Just as Apostle Peter demonstrated an uncommon level of anointing, so did Stephen. God always has those who operate at a higher standard of His grace.

Our churches today have perverted the office of the deacon and turned it into a corporate setting of secular board rooms where decisions are made at the expense of the advancement of the Kingdom. *"Men chosen by men to serve men will always serve themselves"*.

The Deacon

My father is a godly man. I will always identify his life as that of a servant. He is the one I first heard cry out *"here I am Lord, send me"*. He taught me the fear of God and he actually put the fear of God in me. He is a man of very few words, but the words that he speaks are very profound. I confess I always feared him because of his physical stature and his God fearing approach dealing with issues that concerned my life. When he spoke, "it was an E. F. Hutton moment".

> *He who has knowledge spares his words, And a man of understanding is of a calm spirit.* **Proverbs 17:27**

I recognize the season and time of his remaining years and embrace the commitment of his love and devotion shared in the lives of so many that he has touched. The angels of God have been summoned. His work is finished above regret. I recall at the time of my Mother's departure she said *"I have no regrets but if there is any regret it would be if there was any good that I could have done and I did not do it, that I regret"*. What a powerful legacy and shoes too large for me to fill. I pray for God's grace to sustain me in the path of excellence that the testimony of my faith will echo that level of faithfulness.

My Father is a deacon in the Church; a truly ordained and anointed deacon sent to the Body of Christ. He is not just any deacon, but a deacon that operates in the powers of Stephen. He was anointed to do exploits, operating with uncommon powers above the expectations of men who were satisfied with the daily distribution of serving tables. Where others limited their service inside the sanctuary, he went where there was a demand for his gift.

His first lesson to me was the power of fasting. When my younger brother was born, he subsequently had a defect in his body. The doctors had given up hope and told my parents of the consequence, very dire consequence. There was nothing else that man could do. My father took God at his word and began to fast and pray. As scripture says, some things of this kind require fasting and prayer even our unbelief. The result gave birth to the miraculous! My brother was healed and made whole by the power of God.

A demonstration of God's anointing at that level is spiritually impacting and will alter anyone's belief. My father believed the scripture and tested God at His word. It transformed his life and he has never looked back. Subsequently, there have been many testimonies of the healing power of God that flowed through him. He has touched the lives of so many and dedicated his service to raising young men of faith. It is my desire, God willing, to write a fuller testimony of how God used his gifts to bring healing and hope to his generation.

My father knows the power of prayer and taught us the relevance of prayer in our lives. He has a love for God and his family to the likes of which I have not seen demonstrated anywhere else. I call him *"The Deacon";* the true deacon; one that bears testimony of the resurrection power that raised Jesus from the dead. I do not know the moment that he will cry out like Stephen *"Lord receive my spirit",* but I am rested that the same power that raised Jesus from the dead is fully capable to raise up our mortal bodies. My hearts desire is to receive a portion of his life above the measure I have already received. It is my inheritance; not money or any materialistic gain but the testimonies that filled his life. Just as Elisha desired to receive a double portion of Elijah's mantle, I also desire the spiritual inheritance of so great a mantle of faith to replicate at the highest level the fulfillment of God's desire in my life that will carry further the legacy of hope.

I have never in all my years heard my father speak inappropriately. His words were always seasoned with grace. It was a reflection of the maturity and love that exuded from within him. I remember a time when he was travailing in the spirit concerning some practices that had taken root in the church and how the elders were being displaced, those who had given their lives preparing a foundation for the coming generation. I knew how heavy this laid upon his heart when he said to me words I have never heard him utter before. He said *"I have never seen so many stupid Christians in all my life".* I was confounded but I felt his passion. It reminded me of the passage of scripture when Jesus came down from the Mount of Transfiguration to find His disciples in confusion; contending with the world. There are times that we as believers will be or have been confronted with the same challenge. There are some of us who have encountered the intimacy of His presence on top of the mountain and having to leave that place was very difficult to do.

> *And when He came to the disciples, He saw a great multitude around them, and scribes disputing with them. [15]Immediately, when they saw Him, all the people were greatly amazed, and running to Him, greeted Him. [16]And He asked the scribes, "What are you discussing with them?" [17]Then one of the crowd answered and said, "Teacher, I brought You my son, who has a mute spirit. [18]And wherever it seizes him, it throws him down; he foams at the mouth, gnashes his teeth, and becomes rigid. So I spoke to Your disciples, that they should cast it out, but they could not.* **Mark 9:14-19**

The mountain is not where we live. It is a place of visitation for the experience of a divine encounter. After being in His presence, we must come down from our elevation to contend with the things of this world. What we have received, so freely should we give. What God gives us is not for ourselves but for the world that is waiting which He desires to reclaim. *"The whole earth is groaning, waiting for the manifestations of the sons of God."*

After secret communion in the presence of the Lord, men are more attracted to you because of the anointing that remains upon you. As the scripture says in verse 15, *"they will run to you"*. You become recognized in the company of men because of the anointing that readily identifies you as a difference maker. Jesus found His disciples in dispute with the Scribes. The lack of anointing will always leave you in a place of dispute. What was the dispute? It is the same dispute the Church is in today, spiritual inaptness; the inability of the Disciples of Christ to bring healing and deliverance to the hurting. Why couldn't they cast out the spirit that possessed the young man after his father had faith enough to bring him? When the Church consumes itself with materialism and secular things, it renders itself powerless; absent of the anointing that is purposed to demonstrate the power of faith. The love of Christ will be shelved with no expression of His compassion.

I believe that much of the Kingdom still remains bound by the forces of darkness. These forces represented in our time are in bondage to the traditions of man living in the tolerance of the word but denying the anointing that is purposed to bring about healing to our generation. Remember Lazarus who received resurrection power but was still bound? That's indicative of the Church today refusing to change; still bound, stuck in the limited performances of yesterday! Hands and feet still bound without the ability to carry out the requirements of faith to bring reconciliation into our times. Only when we are free from the power that holds us captive are we free to release God's expressions from our gifts.

Chapter 14

Prophetic Purpose and Vision

The LORD of hosts has sworn, saying, Surely, as I have thought, so it shall come to pass, And as I have purposed, so it shall stand. **Isaiah 14:24**

The most important element of prophetic purpose is "*vision*". Purpose is an indication of what God intends to accomplish out of our lives that was assigned to us at birth. It justifies our existence for the reason we are here. It also represents the evidence that concludes the challenge of our search for identity and brings definition to accurately appropriate what is to be our destiny. Purpose is the voice of vision indicating God's intended performance. It reveals the path to a destination; where God purpose to target His energy and a discovery of how He chooses to use us.

> *Shall a trumpet be blown in the city, and the people not be afraid? Shall there be evil in a city, and the LORD hath not done it? Surely the Lord GOD will do nothing, but he revealeth his secret unto his servants the prophets. The lion hath roared, who will not fear? The Lord GOD hath spoken, who can but prophesy?* **Amos 3:6-8**

Defining the Purpose

Purpose is what defines and drives our vision. Defining the purpose is the most critical aspect of identifying God's prophetic season. Sometimes, this can be the most challenging experience we endeavor to pursue. If we are not careful, the patience that is required will never be developed in us if we do not possess the patience to wait. Our lives are hidden in Christ Jesus and we are placed in obscurity where we will remain until He brings us forth.

Discernment of the signs of our time will give us an indication of what God's desire is in the earth. The heavens and the earth testify of His revelation. There is a parallel of spiritual and natural manifestations coexisting at the same time. What is birth in the spirit will manifest to our natural senses pre-existing revelations of our time.

> *And in the morning, It will be foul weather today, for the sky is red and threatening. Hypocrites! You know how to discern the face of the sky, but you cannot discern the signs of the times.* **Matthew 16:3**

Proverbs teaches us that *"if we don't understand the purpose of a thing; its original intended application; we will squander the appropriations meant for our achievement"*. Jesus has given every man talents, gifts and a measure of faith to extrapolate what He has placed in their heart.

Write the Vision

Without God's prophetic purpose being accurately defined, we cannot access the dimension of prophetic flow emanating from the Spirit of God and operate in the measure of the anointing that He intends to pour into us. In the divine economy of God, he purposes to release all of the resources necessary to bring full resolution to His vision. In the book of Habakkuk, God has established a spiritual protocol to execute His prophetic intent. These processes are required if we are to establish the works of the Kingdom.

> *I will stand upon my watch, and set me upon the tower, and will watch to see what he will say unto me, and what I shall answer when I am reproved. And the LORD answered me, and said; Write the vision, and make it plain upon tables, that he may run that readeth it. For the vision is yet for an appointed time, but at the end it shall speak, and not lie: though it tarry, wait for it; because it will surely come, it will not tarry.* **Habakkuk 2:1-3**

Watching and waiting presents opportunities to discover and appropriate the vision the Lord reveals. As we position ourselves with a readiness to execute His judgments, we will be able to render an answer when He speaks. He will reprove us in our preparation to implement what He says and what we hear. We are never to lose the record of His testimony. There is a time stamp to every vision that will determine the time and season of His words. Just as Moses on top of Mount Sinai, the record was recorded. It must be accurately written to the order that the Lord reveals. Our night season is a battle ground the enemy uses to cause slumber and interruption to keep us from retaining the revelations we receive. I always position myself with a pad and pen to quickly record the things that I see. If not, I am likely to leave out a significant detail.

Attend and Incline

> My son, give attention to my words; Incline your ear to my sayings. *21Do not let them depart from your eyes; Keep them in the midst of your heart; For they are life to those who find them, And health to all their flesh.* **Proverbs 4:20-22**

The role of the prophetic church require that we not only "*attend*" to those things that God has spoken (Logos) but we must have an "*inclining*" ear to hear what the Spirit of the Living God has to say (Rhema). Logos is the written testimony of God's performance in our history that testifies of His future intentions. Rhema is a path into the operation of God in our present life and future hopes powered by revelation knowledge of the spirit. To incline is to look up; to attend is to look down. We have to develop an accurate balance in our motivation in pursuing God in prayer; getting into His presence, waiting on Him and studying His Word to make the proper discernment of His will.

We have become masters of the written word; the logos. There are libraries full of revelation of the scriptures. In our nobility searching the scriptures, revelation is almost a daily adventure seeking the discovery of things that were hidden before.

> These were more nobler than those in Thessalonica, in that they received the word with all readiness of mind, and searched the scriptures daily, whether those things were so. **Acts 17:11**

Proceeding Onward

Abraham was 99 years old when God decided to change His name from Abram to Abraham. This gives every indication that we can not confine the time and season of God. So the proper response to our expectation of God intervening into our affairs is to offer Him obedience at all times. God had prophesied to Abraham in Haran, the land of his father, that He would give him revelation of His future intentions and that He would also make him a great nation. Isn't it exciting that God will make for us those things that He chooses to fulfill His desire that are purposed to be a blessing to us and our generation? Abraham was 75 years old when he received his prophecy. It took another 24 years for the revelation of God's intention to fully unfold, but it only took one year from the time that God prophesied of Isaac for the promise to manifest.

Hebrews 10:35 says *"You have need of patience, so that after you have done the will of God, you may receive the promise"*. We have a need to allow the Lord to fulfill His promises in our lives. It will require patience and obedience. Patience is a time given for our obedience to be worked out; a time to prove our faith that we have done the will of God. The promises given can not be apprehended until this process is complete. Our endurance must be proven as an exhibition of our trust. If you have ever gotten stuck in your spiritual walk and you don't know which way to go or what to do, I might suggest you go back to the last word the Lord instructed you to do. You will not be able to see your way forward into the direction for your future if it is dependent upon completion of past instructions.

Every promise made from God is conditional to our obedience. The Lord told Abraham *"walk before Me and be perfect and I will make My covenant between you and Me"*. Abraham received the condition for the promise. Be Perfect! Perfect is not in the manner of your adherence to the laws that are written in tablets of stone but to the specifics of His instructions; *"did you do what I instructed you to do"*?

There comes a time when our obedience to perfect the word that has been given to us will be tested. If He chooses to alter our path *"we must allow Him to speak beyond the point of where we last heard Him"*. The Lord is faithful to fulfill His promises; indirectly or directly. The indirect way leads to a path of learning and development of a testimony. The children of Israel wandered in the wilderness for forty years of testimony before indirectly entering into the promise. I would hope it will not take us that long to perfect obedience. David was by no means a perfect man. He had done some wicked things in his life time and paid a heavy price for the flaws in his character and integrity. But he was a man after God's own heart and God chose to use him in spite of his flaws and weaknesses. God wanted to use his obedience. If He chooses to use a "donkey", certainly he can use you and me.

God gave Abraham instructions to offer Isaac as a sacrifice. Abraham would be tested after already being separated from the life of his son Ishmael. The thought may have challenged his faith and he may have felt the price was too costly to continue his walk of faith, but he had trust in the outcome of his obedience. God gave Abraham specific instructions.

Now it came to pass after these things that God tested Abraham, and said to him, "Abraham!" And he said, "Here I am." ²Then He said, Take now your son, your only son Isaac, whom you love, and go to the land of Moriah, and offer him there as a burnt offering on one of the mountains of which I shall tell you. **Genesis 22:1-2**

Abraham's hearing would be tested to determine the resolve in his heart. It was a choice to make that would filter his passion of love for his son from his instructions of faith. Our rewards emanate from our obedience and Abraham was no different. There are times in our inner conflict wrestling with our passion and God's instruction we can miss the details of what He said. The consequence of our obedience will then be rendered only in part. Abraham was instructed to offer Isaac as a sacrifice *"on one of the mountains which I shall tell you"*. God had already had a ram in the bush waiting for him on top of *"this mountain"* in the land of *"Moriah"*. If Abraham had not followed the instructions given, he could have ended up on the wrong mountain with no sacrifice in exchange for the promised life of Isaac. It would have had an impact on your future and mine. But Abraham moved in obedience in the trusted judgments of God, recognizing that Isaac was the sacrifice and the promise carrying the hope of generations to come.

Lay not thine hand upon the lad, neither do thou any thing unto him: for now I know that thou fearest God, seeing thou hast not withheld thy son, thine only son from me.
Genesis 22:12

The principle: *"Fear God and keep His commandments, for this is the whole duty of Man"*. The ultimate we can offer God is the sacrifice of our obedience; *"the whole of it"*. Obedience requires an ability to separate the hidden treasures of our heart of things we value the most from the demands of faith. The resolute of our faith should echo the words of Jesus, "who is my mother, who is my brother". Faith's destination exceeds familiarity.

> *Yea doubtless, and I count all things but loss for the excellency of the knowledge of Christ Jesus my Lord: for whom I have suffered the loss of all things, and do count them but dung, that I may win Christ, And be found in him, not having mine own righteousness, which is of the law, but that which is through the faith of Christ, the righteousness which is of God by faith: That I may know him, and the power of his resurrection, and the fellowship of his sufferings, being made conformable unto his death; If by any means I might attain unto the resurrection of the dead. Not as though I had already attained, either were already perfect: but I follow after, if that I may apprehend that for which also I am apprehended of Christ Jesus. Brethren, I count not myself to have apprehended: but this one thing I do, forgetting those things which are behind, and reaching forth unto those things which are before, I press toward the mark for the prize of the high calling of God in Christ Jesus.* **Phil 3:8-14**

The Price for Change

In a vision in the night, the Lord spoke a Word to me: *"Envy not your oppressor and choose none of his ways"*. A time of change had emerged. A new path was chartered with different choices to consider. The path carved out before me restricted the ways to my past. I realized that I would suffer the lost of things around me with instructions not to envy the separation. I was to leave the arena of comfort that had become so familiar to me, so trusting and so needed in my life. But for the greater call of faith, the requirement of change would test my obedience in the undiscovered path ahead.

Abraham was instructed to leave his roots, kinfolk and the environment of familiarity. The furtherance of what God intended for his life would be predicated on his obedience to faith. The price for change can be very demanding. It forces us with unique choices, if we truly are to emerge as a prophetic people pursuing the destiny of faith. When Jesus was preaching and his family came on the *"outside of what he was doing"* trying to impede on His mission, He did not hesitate to respond with His commitment of faith which should be an example to us all.

> *For whosoever shall do the will of my Father which is in heaven, the same is my brother, and sister, and mother..... He that loveth father or mother more than me is not worthy of me: and he that loveth son or daughter more than me is not worthy of me. And he that taketh not his cross, and followeth after me, is not worthy of me.*
> **Matthew 12:46; Matt. 10:37-38**

Leave Your Country-Your Kindred-Your Father

It is very difficult for a prophet, for that matter prophetic people to establish God's order where the spirit of familiarity prevails. Our greatest challenges are instigated by those that have close connections to us and offer the greatest threat. David made reference to the fact regarding his persecutions that "he could have understood it if it had been anyone else other than his brother".

> *A friend loveth at all times, and a brother is born for adversity.* **Proverbs 17:17**

Close Ties Breeds Contempt

Contempt usually comes from those who have close pre-existing connections into your life. For the most part, when contempt arises, it is an indication of an illegal connection. Contempt is the feeling or attitude of regarding someone or something as inferior or worthless. There are four levels of contempt; disrespect, despise, dishonor and disgrace. The intensity of contempt leads to open disrespect or willful disobedience of authority. Usually the one that is the object of contempt is scorned.

> *My friends scorn me: my eyes pour out tears to God. Oh that one might plead for a man with God, as a man pleads for his neighbour!* **Job 16:20-21**

Change Produces a New Level of Trust

The principles gleaned from the testimony of Abraham are attributes indicative of our sacrifices of faith and obedience. But there is something much more impacting.

Abraham personified a willingness to accept the things of God at any cost. For the advancing of the Kingdom, it will require a separation from every connection of familiarity. Any connection to your destiny that God has not assigned can not be incorporated into your success. Our eagerness and zeal at times can impede our progression if we are not vigilant of the forces sent to us as agents of despondency.

Abraham was given the instructions to leave his country and kindred which were not purposed to be his inheritance. God's desire was to make him a father of many nations. Abraham could not establish the order of God under a pre-existing authority. There had to be separation from his father's house for the emergence of nations that would come from his seed. Often times we choose to implement prophetic instructions with old solutions and ill advised spiritual connections that can render itself as a gross impediment to Kingdom building.

Our obedience to faith is a requirement of the life of every Believer. But there is a higher sacrifice than faith; it is the price of love. The love of our Father should be of greater value than our secret treasures. At the command of His Word, our hearts will be tested at the core of our inner recesses. If the fuel of our passions burns brighter than the Light of the Spirit within, it will delay our acquisition to faith and shadow our dreams and aspirations waiting in the path ahead. Tend the fire of God's light with your wick always trimmed to set ablaze the world with the power of your faith. As a beacon of light on a thousand hills, let the radiance of your love be a flame of life.

¹⁵ So when they had eaten breakfast, Jesus said to Simon Peter, "Simon, son of Jonah, do you love Me more than these?" He said to Him, "Yes, Lord; You know that I love You." He said to him, "Feed My lambs." ¹⁶ He said to him again a second time, "Simon, son of Jonah, do you love Me?" He said to Him, "Yes, Lord; You know that I love You." He said to him, "Tend My sheep." ¹⁷ He said to him the third time, "Simon, son of Jonah do you love Me?" Peter was grieved because He said to him the third time, "Do you love Me?" And he said to Him, "Lord, You know all things; You know that I love You." Jesus said to him, "Feed My sheep. ¹⁸ Most assuredly, I say to you, when you were younger, you girded yourself and walked where you wished; but when you are old, you will stretch out your hands, and another will gird you and carry you where you do not wish." ¹⁹ This He spoke, signifying by what death he would glorify God. And when He had spoken this, He said to him, "Follow Me." **John 21:15-19**

Words of Wisdom

By Inez Ham Wingate
October 11, 1998

- Even roses grow amidst thorns, but the thorns can not destroy the fragrance of a rose or its beauty.

- Never let the enemy control your behavior, nor let him know what you are thinking at any time.

- Don't be discouraged if the sun does not seem to be shining in your life. Always remember, the clouds do not destroy the sun or the rays. It only blocks them for awhile.

- Laughter in life is like the seasoning in food. It gives flavor to it.

- Begin your walk each day with the Lord before you, and the Lord will show you favor in whatever you do in that day.

- Hate is like an insect in the middle of a fruit. If it remains there, it will eventually destroy it.

- Love heals; hate destroys.

- When you have nothing else to give, give of yourself.

- Think your way out of sickness, once your mind is healed, your body is sure to follow.

- The Joy of the Lord is your strength. Rejoice always in the Lord.

- Seek to learn something positive each day then put it to practice.

- Never ask why am I suffering, but rather why are we suffering; because everyone is suffering directly or indirectly.

The Beaten Path
Kofi

I traveled far in the night to reach you here at the dawning of light; there is a message for you, listen to me all the way through.

Moses is dead just waiting on you, he had the law until grace came true. The law is dead and religion too, leave the past before your time is through.

Religion only bears the testimony of where God has been, It only has power for the redemption of sin; on the beaten path.

It speaks the knowledge of what He is, never contacting His presence to experience His power where He is; on the beaten path.

It is a monument full of expressions of what He did, not the revelation of who He is; on the beaten path.

There you will find relics of the past and ceremonies that testify and rituals to ensue a path to the past; on the beaten path.

It is a house gone empty with no path to the future; all the people gone and nowhere to enter; on the beaten path.

It bears the testimony of His past occupation; a stream that once was a river of life, now has become a place of continual strife; on the beaten path.

A place locked into the beginning until yesterday, wanting to move forward but always moving backwards into; the beaten path.

A place of reluctance with the challenge of new. A home for the rested with no comfort to the weary; on the beaten path.

Back and forth, coming and going, there is nothing new; just a reinvention of the same with new crutches for the lame; on the beaten path.

It is the parched land of man with no river to sail a ship into the deeper dimensions of God's grace, how I long for another taste before it turn into waste; on the beaten path.

It is a ship with paddles of wood that can not survive the turbulence of the deep. Carrying the burdens of time you need not keep; on the beaten path.

It moves amongst the shallow shores connecting with ships of its kind. Now it is time for a celebration, once a month we come together and share bread and wine remembering in time; on the beaten path.

A path to nowhere that has already been, a path locked into the circles of time struggling to break free, locked into the cycle of my defeat; on the beaten path.

It is the path of merchants selling their goods of fish dinners and chicken delights, it's simply good and you will agree, but my desire is to go much deeper into the deep blue sea; on the beaten path.

With no power to get to the other side and no faith to walk on water and more water than we can drink, we are stuck; on the beaten path.

Off the beaten path is the pathfinder of our future, leading us forward in grace unforeseen. Faith and charity with the light of God's Spirit will bring us hope and we will never fear it; "off the beaten path".

Please let me out, I don't want to go in. I don't want to go nowhere I have already been, I want to move forward where I have never been; off the beaten path.

Hear me now or hear me late, I guess you wonder why I just can't wait, lets make sure we got things straight, get off the beaten path before it's too late; off the beaten path.

I will share with you now or share with you then, some place in time I don't know when, this I'm sure we will share again; off the beaten path.

Come go with me, I'll take you there, it's a place where you'll have no care, where we are going is some place far, it's a place where I've always been, this I know there is no sin; *off the beaten path.*

You'll experience as never before. The love of my Father who loves to share, a crown of glory you'll always wear; off the beaten path.

It's time for me to go back into the light, I only came for just a few moments of sight, I have no clothes only a garment of light; off the beaten path.

I need no ticket to take me there, The wings of angels are already here, I'm building my mansion with no room to spare, you must see for yourself the crown waiting for you to wear,

Peace and love to all of you all that I have said is really true, follow me there leave this old town, there's really nothing worth losing your crown.

I'll fly away only this time I will stay, you won't see me again on this side of time, I gave you the message in what I was sent to do, yesterday's gone and today will soon be too.

Now it is time to say goodbye, I'll spread my wings and take my flight; heaven is waiting I can't be late, I'll tell HIM what I just told you, all that HE said I repeated to you. The bells of time continue to ring, it time for me to hear the angels sing.

Are they ministers of Christ? I speak as a fool I am more: in labors more abundant, in stripes above measure, in prisons more frequently, in deaths often. ²⁴*From the Jews five times I received forty stripes minus one.* ²⁵*Three times I was beaten with rods; once I was stoned; three times I was shipwrecked; a night and a day I have been in the deep;* ²⁶*in journeys often, in perils of waters, in perils of robbers, in perils of my own countrymen, in perils of the Gentiles, in perils in the city, in perils in the wilderness, in perils in the sea, in perils among false brethren;* ²⁷*in weariness and toil, in sleeplessness often, in hunger and thirst, in fastings often, in cold and nakedness* ²⁸*besides the other things, what comes upon me daily: my deep concern for all the churches.* **2 Corinthians 11:23-28**

Selah

References

All scripture references attributed to: Biblegateway.com
   King James
   New King James

Definitions researched at Dictionary.com

Strong's Exhaustive Concordance
   Thomas Nelson Publishers 1990

Thanks to the Spirit of Christ for wisdom, revelation, faith, knowledge, understanding, dreams, visions and a light unto my path for directions.

Email: clariongate@msn.com
www.sankofastar.com